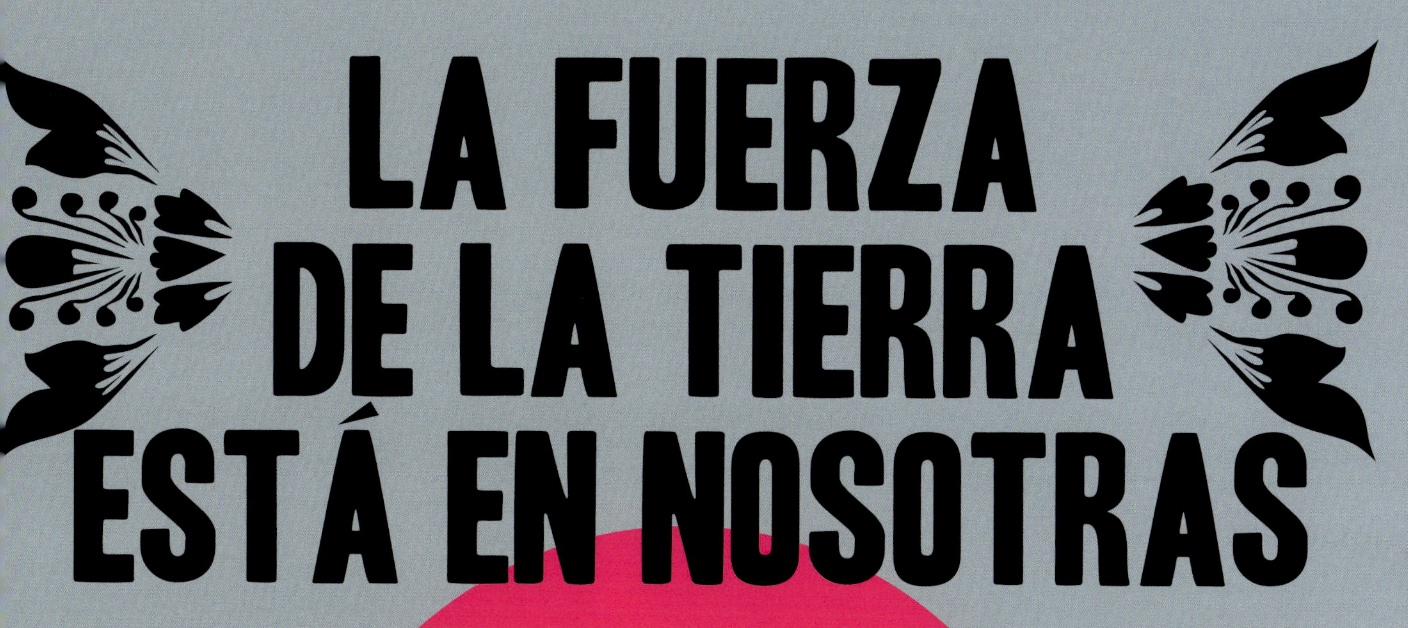

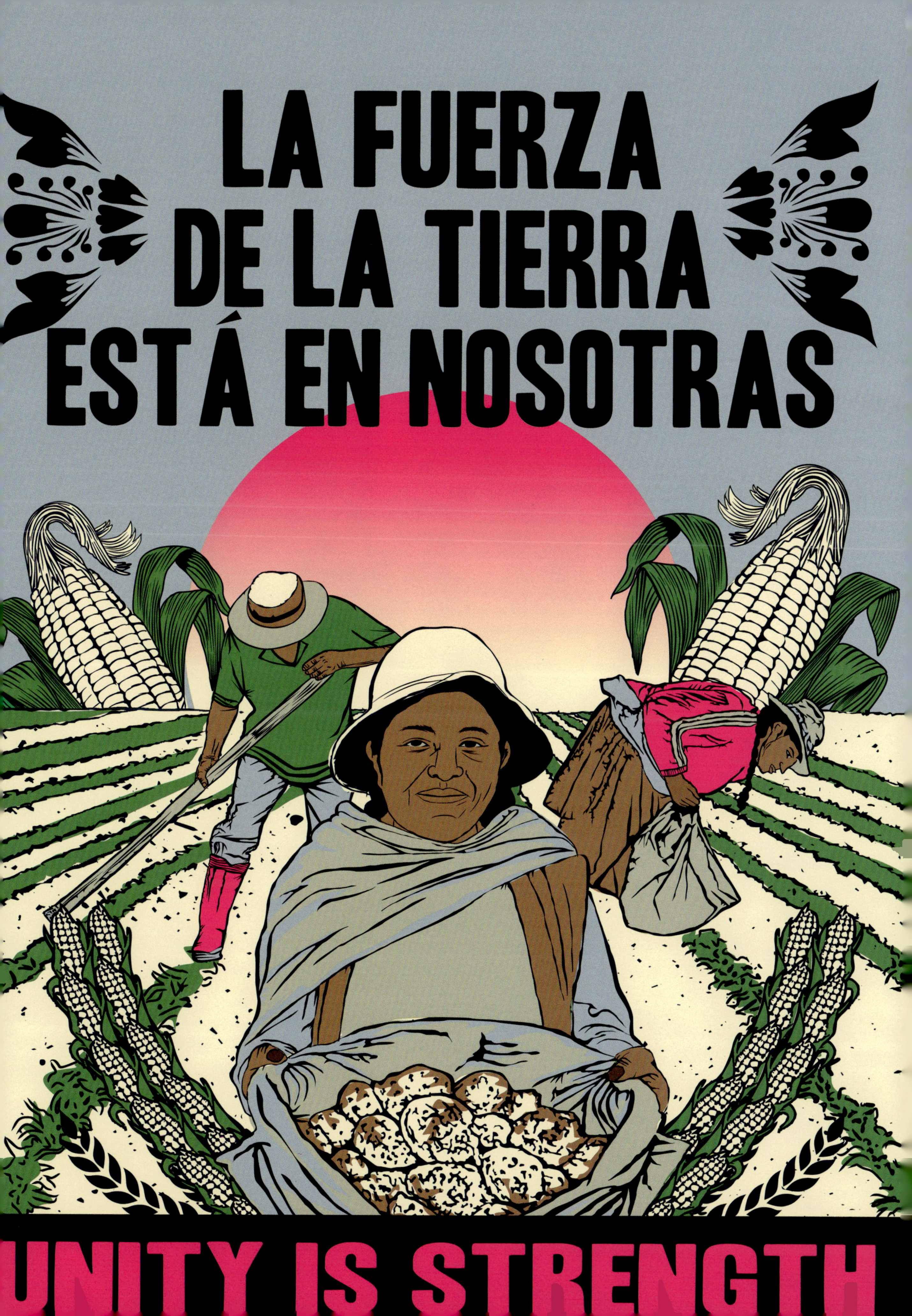
LA FUERZA
DE LA TIERRA
ESTÁ EN NOSOTRAS
UNITY IS STRENGTH

DEFENDER LA AMAZONIA ES DEFENDER LA VIDA

NO MAS DEFENSORES ASESINADOS

FALSE DRAGONS

Alice Sparkly Kat

There's an old adage in astrology: "as above, so below." The idea is that things bigger and higher than us, things like the weather, the seasons, and the stars which chart the weather and the seasons, impact the ecosystems in which people and other life forms live. The second part of the adage, which goes "as below, so above" is often left out. The adage is true. If plants didn't exist, then the earth would not be so full of water and our skies would be barren. Living organisms, even though we are much smaller than whole solar systems, have a huge impact on our own environments. Both types of movement, from high to low and from small to big, create energy. Energy is created from movement. "As above, so below; as below, so above" speaks to equilibrium.

In Chinese myth, the issue of scale is dealt with using dragons. Dragons can shrink to a size that is as small as an earthworm and grow to become as big as the universe. The milky way is a dragon. So are rivers and the rain. Dragons sleep in the mountains. A glacier is a sleeping dragon and an avalanche is one waking up. A trickle of water running along the stem of a stalk is also a dragon.

There are two words for power in Chinese: 势 and 力. 力 deals with physical strength. The more you consume, the more 力 you have. An older version of the character shows a hand plowing a field. 势 has to do with position and also means either posture or momentum. While living beings like humans or cows have 力, creatures like dragons wield 势. Humans and cows eat to power our bodies and we plow the fields to influence our surroundings. Dragons don't eat. Dragons flow from a high point, usually the summit of a mountain or a plateau, to lower ground. Instead of using calories to power themselves, dragons use positioning to gain momentum. Every ecological system and every culture is born out of some dragon or body of flowing freshwater. The weather replenishes the glaciers in the mountains by way of evaporating groundwater. Every spring, the dragons wake up and fill the fields with water. Energy, in this system, is something that dragons give us. Dragons give us energy when small dragons in the form of river tributaries or creeks create fertile fields and power agriculture. The big dragon of the milky way gives us energy by creating the seasons and the sun. River dragons give us energy for travel by pushing boats with their currents. The delta of the river, where it flows into the sea, is called the dragon's breath.

Water doesn't just shape life. As below, so above. Trees play a role in shaping rivers by clenching around dirt with their roots. Where a river meanders and whether it becomes a floodplain or narrow current depends on trees. Our rivers wouldn't look the way they do without trees. People also shape rivers to some extent. For thousands of years, people have been building structures to control floods.

Even though I haven't mentioned it explicitly, you might have already guessed that a dragon is a metaphor for water. But a dragon isn't just water.

Micah S. Muscolino writes about a battle that took place in Henan province towards the beginning of World War II. The KMT, which was on the verge of collapse and trying to flee from the Japanese to Chongqing, tried to buy time for itself using the scorched earth policy of changing the direction of the Yellow River. Ancient dykes were destroyed. These dykes were holding the Yellow River in place. This is a river that is sometimes called the people's sorrow because it likes to change course so often, destroying villages and fields. The Yellow River is yellow because it is full of silt. As silt deposits into one part of the river, the riverbed is pushed up until the water is diverted in another direction. This is why the Yellow River is so unpredictable.

In the floods of 1938 alone, an estimated one million people died. Most of them were peasant farmers. Many more would die in subsequent years. Between 1938 to 1942, the KMT and Japan would each try to unleash the force of the river towards enemy lines. Each side would enlist labor from starving farmers whose fields had been ruined by floodwaters. Because people going through famine are unable to build sturdy infrastructure and because the Yellow River is uncontrollable, the new and shoddily built dykes would fail again and again. The flooding caused food shortages, labor shortages (men left home and agricultural work to join the military in exchange for food), disease, and locusts (locusts swarm when the ecology is disturbed). By 1943, around three million people had died.

When Chiang Kai-shek gave the order to change the course of the Yellow River, he was trying to become a dragon. Like Chiang Kai-shek, every contemporary ruler has tried to become a dragon in some way. Living people eat food to receive energy. Governing organizations position themselves in various ways to acquire power (dragons flow from high to low). Living people shape our environments by working for a wage. Nations incentivize behavior by issuing currency (dragons give water and the means for life). By using nationalism, nations stage themselves as the source or narrator of a culture. Even though economies are sets of rules, markets are viewed and treated as naturally occurring or spontaneously regenerating things by the people who run them.

But even though every contemporary ruler has tried to become a dragon, none of them have really succeeded. Dragons are replenished by the weather. To my knowledge, no economy runs on the weather. No ruler has been able to control the weather.

In the past, the materials that powered colonialism were mostly narcotics: opium, tobacco, tea, and coffee. Today, imperialism extracts energy conducting materials: oil, cobalt, and natural gas. Oil and natural gas are burned to create energy. Cobalt is used to stabilize batteries. When people use gas powered or battery powered tools, we are able to access and use more energy than just the calories burned by our metabolisms. Most of these energy holding materials or mediums of power begin under the ground in poor countries and end up inside of machines owned by rich countries.

Subjects of imperialist countries are told that extracted materials will make our lives easier and more efficient, that these extracted materials will make us feel as though we are not powered by our metabolism but by slopes. We, too, want to be like dragons who don't eat and flow from high to low. This is where dragons become mystical instead of geographical. We imagine that we are dragons.

Nations with big economies and powerful militaries must go through great lengths to compete for energy. African and Arab leaders are assassinated to make way for dictators friendly to imperialist interests. Most of the oil, gas, and minerals of the world don't go to any living person regardless of location or citizenship. Most resources are spent on the most expensive, wasteful, and destructive organism in the world—the military.

The military is the most expensive governmental instrument. The US spends more on its military than all other public sectors combined. The goal of the military is to literally waste lives. Militaries exist to kill. Resources within the military are usually wasted. Much of the food used to feed soldiers spoils enroute because it has to travel such great lengths. Militaries also bring catastrophic harm to their own environment by use of missiles, bombs, and chemical weapons. The more energy a military uses, the more it also needs. The more a military or police entity exploits, the more energy it needs to consume in order to keep exploiting.

Today, the world is running out of oil and minerals. Oil is destined to run out in 2052. Known sources of cobalt are also destined to run dry in around four or five decades. Some of our rivers, including the Colorado River, will dry up even earlier.

Muscolino describes the five years between 1938 and 1943 in Henan as an energy crisis. Back then, inadequate crop yields meant that people and animals could not eat enough to power their metabolisms. Everyone in the region, including civilians, soldiers, animals, and pathogens, competed for energy. Humans ate dogs but dogs also ate humans. Soldiers raided farmers for food. Bacteria and viruses that flourished due to the floodwaters and decaying corpses competed with their human and animal hosts for survival. Muscolino describes the situation of the people back then in these terms: they had to compete with both macroparasites (militaries) and microparasites (pathogens).

Today, Henan treats the catastrophes of the past as something that has been overcome simply because it happened under the jurisdiction of the KMT. This couldn't be further from the truth. The energy crisis is not over. It has grown more problematic. More and more people—in Congo, in Gaza, in Mindanao—all compete with imperialism and pathogens for survival.

In the past, rulers portrayed themselves as gods. We judge ancient people for believing that their kings delivered messages from their gods. How could some power tripping asshole be a god? It's not like that guy was the one to breathe life into your lungs. But our contemporary rulers also use powerful symbols. They dress themselves in the emblems of power. They name rivers after themselves, conflating a river which is the source of life with a national identity. Those rivers become symbols that are infused with national feeling.

But a river isn't a national symbol. A river is a body of flowing freshwater. Rivers make life possible. This is something that no imperial power has been able to do. No imperial power is able to create energy. Oil and natural gas are formed when the earth puts high heat and pressure on the decomposing bodies of marine animals that lived before the dinosaurs. These are the great dragons of the past. Cobalt is more mysterious. Some geologists think that cobalt is found in such high amounts in Congo because there must have been some kind of asteroid at some point. If this is the case, then cobalt comes from the big dragon in the sky—the milky way.

A dragon is more than just a natural being or a mystical being. A dragon is an imaginary being. It takes imagination to create a dragon. Dragons are created when living beings collaborate with water. If a dragon is a metaphor, then it is a metaphor for power.

Power is just the distribution of energy. Power forms when water flows from high to low. It forms when the small works on the big. As above, so below; as below, so above. Power is the ability to use energy for the sake of life. Power is inherent in agriculture. Our rulers pretend to be dragons but they've never been able to generate life. They can regulate life or control it but no one has ever been able to generate life on command. As below, so above: oil, minerals, food, and life matter flow from workers to rulers. As above, so below: in return, the people face police and military. Life flows one way and death another. If there is injustice in this exchange, then we will face an energy crisis because of it.

LIFE-THREATENING

LIFE RAFTS

Images by the Turkish Coast Guard and Hibai Arbide

Hibai Arbide

112
ACİL
KB-4310
SAHİL GÜVENLİK

A LANDING

At midnight between the 9th and 10th of February 2023, an 8-metre-long black dinghy ran aground on some rocks at Chrissi Ammos beach in northern Lesbos, Greece. Chrissi Ammos means golden sands, but the dinghy's passengers could not discern the colour of the land. Although full moon had been five days earlier, it still reflected enough light for them to disembark and run into the forest in the hope that they wouldn't be stopped by the coastguards. The wind was getting stronger; the sea was choppy, and waves were breaking everywhere. The 30-horsepower Yamaha engine was clearly insufficient for a boat of that size and had been pushed to the limit over the 18 kilometres that separated this point of the island from Turkey because, what's more, the boat was completely overloaded.

It was carrying 45 people from Eritrea, Yemen and Libya. As soon as they arrived, several of them called the emergency numbers of lawyers and NGOs that assist refugees to declare their intention to apply for asylum in Greece. Yemen is at war, Libya is one of the most dangerous countries in the world, and Eritrea is an even more isolated regime than North Korea or Turkmenistan; they clearly qualified for international protection. The lawyers informed the police of the group's arrival by email and that their intention was to seek asylum. Humanitarian organisations must immediately inform the authorities when they become aware of a landing because in Greece, since 2018, rescues and the provision of any other assistance on beaches are prohibited. Helping these people, for example, by saving their lives in a shipwreck without informing the authorities carries a 10-year prison sentence – it is a crime of "facilitating illegal immigration".

At around 1.30 am, about an hour after the authorities learned that 45 people had arrived from Turkey to save their lives in Europe, two journalists arrived at Chrissi Ammos. One of them was this author, who has never told this story before. At the junction of two dirt roads just after the turn-off from the road to the beach, a car flashed its lights twice as the journalists passed. The journalists didn't understand what it meant. When they reached the beach, barely 500 metres further on, the wind was the only thing they could hear. On the shore, next to the rocks, there were dozens of life jackets next to the dinghy. There were also half-opened backpacks with food, personal belongings, phone chargers and wallets that appeared to have been emptied of documents and money. They found a couple of documents in Arabic and Turkish, as well as wet sheets of paper with notes in the Ethiopian alphabet, probably in the Tigrinya language. They were the traces of the passengers who had all disappeared.

At 10 am, the journalists returned to the scene. In the light of day, they found more life jackets, leading them to a clearing in the forest next to the beach where several backpacks and travel bags had been dumped in the undergrowth. It was obvious that someone had opened them to rummage through them. There were also open wallets from which money, if there had been any, and documents had been taken. Clothes, food, water bottles, toothbrushes. Alongside the travellers' belongings were several pairs of latex gloves. It was, without a doubt, the scene of a search. Someone had used those gloves to search the bags and, most likely, the bodies of their owners.

At 7:25 on the 10th of February, a TCSG-907 Turkish Coast Guard patrol boat rescued two groups of shipwrecked people off the coast of Dikili, Izmir province, opposite Lesbos, in two life rafts. The group consisted of 45 people of Eritrean, Yemeni and Libyan nationality. How 45 people who had set foot on EU soil ended up adrift in Turkish waters is not as difficult a mystery to solve as it might at first appear.

THE PUSHBACKS

Since March 2020, the Greek coastguard has been systematically carrying out pushbacks from the Greek islands. Although there are records of this illegal practice dating back more than a decade, it wasn't until the New Democracy government came to power that these pushbacks became a structural tool of border policy. There are two main forms. The first occurs when the Greek coastguard intercepts a boat at sea. Often, the uniformed officers in the coastguard patrol boats are accompanied by hooded, armed men dressed in black military-style clothing that is not an official uniform. They break the engine of the boat carrying the migrants, or remove it and throw it into the sea, leaving the inflatable dinghy adrift. Often, to access the engine, they use long metal rods, which are also used to beat the refugees if they get between the hooded men and the engine. Having your children set adrift in a powerless boat with dozens of other people is one of the most horrifying experiences reported by those who come, frequently, directly from war. And yet, the second form of pushback is even more terrifying. It involves the use of life rafts.

The hooded paramilitaries do not only operate at sea; they also seek out newly arrived migrants before they are seen by anyone, especially medical NGOs, lawyers or the UNHCR, in order to detain them – the correct term should be abduct them. If there are inconvenient witnesses, they have no choice but to search the asylum seekers and transfer them to the island's refugee camp. When no one is looking, or when those who are looking are indifferent, they detain the migrants, sometimes at gunpoint, rob them of their belongings, tie their hands with cable ties, beat them in front of their children, and shout at the children themselves. They search the genitals of adults and minors, men and women, looking for hidden money or jewellery; they seldom change gloves from one person to another. Many women report molestation and groping of a sexual nature. They confiscate their phones, keeping the smartphones in good condition. Sometimes, the violence is even crueller. Several Afghan refugees had their faces squashed against a dead dog. A group of young refugees were rescued after spending several days in the forest with their hands tied. A woman died of hypothermia while hiding in a forest in Lesbos. Dozens of men have had their bones broken in beatings intended as a deterrent: tell them what we did to you so that no one else will want to attempt it.

Afterwards, the migrants are transported in unmarked, unregistered vans that speed around the islands. Everyone can see the green and white vans breaking the speed limits and circulating without number plates with a hooded man at the wheel. Everyone except the local authorities and the European border agency, Frontex, which never sees them. Several islands have clandestine detention centres – secret prisons – where migrants spend hours, or days, before being deported. On Kos and Samos, cases of torture have been reported in them. On Lesbos, no one has managed to prove their existence so far. From there, they are picked up in the same unregistered vans. The vans stop at a small wooden jetty, and the migrants are forced onto a Hellenic Coast Guard boat. After a short sail, between half an hour and an hour and a half, close to Turkish waters, the migrants are thrown into an inflatable life raft. They do not board; they are thrown. Fedaa, a Syrian refugee, said, "They threw my young son onto the raft as if he were rubbish." Miriam, a Congolese refugee, described it this way: "They herded us into the boat as if we were sheep. But a shepherd never beats his flock."

More than once, migrants have fallen into the water instead of onto the raft. In 2021, on Lesbos, 11 bodies washed up on the beaches unrelated to any reported shipwreck. The total number for all the islands is unknown. Every year, new floating corpses appear.

Nora Bauckhorn is a Lesbos resident with a long track record in Search and Rescue (SAR) operations and grassroots movements in solidarity with the migrant population. She has a life raft certification and has been trained on how to use them in the event of an emergency. "The first thing to do in a life raft is to open the grab bag containing flares, a line cutter and, most importantly, dimenhydrinate tablets," explains Nora. Unlike boats, the bottom of a life raft is not rigid; it moves around a lot, so the tablets are essential to prevent seasickness. "Without dimenhydrinate in a raft, you get seasick immediately, and the rafts used in pushbacks don't have a grab bag," the rescuer claims.

Liferafts are not navigable; they just float. They cannot be rowed, nor do they have an engine. This means that the only thing you can do is wait. Wait for hours or days until someone comes to rescue you. The rafts Greece uses for pushbacks are made by the company LALIZAS and have a maximum capacity of 6 to 12 people. In October 2023, 33 people were forced to board just one of the rafts. Normally, there's not as many, but the weight limit is almost always exceeded. "A raft is a lifesaver when used in the way it was designed to be used," Nora reminds us, "overloading them is extremely dangerous. In addition to the risk of sinking, filling them with too many people can cause someone to fall into the water or result in crushing injuries. Moving around in such a confined space is difficult enough, even when they are used correctly."

In its section on Corporate Responsibility, LALIZAS assures us that "The LALIZAS group of companies is a firm believer that a healthy company in terms of finances should also be a healthy company in terms of social responsibility. Caring about the environment and our community should not be something that companies do in their 'free time'. That's why we are constantly striving to achieve strategic partnerships with organizations that provide help for those who are in need." Nora is categorical in regard to the possibility that the company is unaware of how the Hellenic Coast Guard uses its products: "At a top-end estimate, each Hellenic Coast Guard vessel could have four life rafts. In reality, there are fewer; one would be enough. Let's assume that each boat replaces them annually, which doesn't make much sense either because you don't have to change them; just ensure they pass an annual inspection. Yet, even based on these assumptions, the company couldn't explain the number of rafts it sells to the State each year."

In 2023, 278 life rafts were used in pushbacks in the Aegean Sea. The year before, it was 553. Each of them has a retail price of more than 1,200 euros. And although a significantly reduced price has been negotiated because of the quantity, we're still talking about hundreds of thousands of euros spent every year on life rafts for the last three years. Doesn't anyone audit the accounts?

The port of Mytilene, the capital of Lesbos, is small and positioned in the centre of the city. In front of the maritime authority building, next to the space reserved for ferries to Turkey, it's not unusual to see burly men out of uniform, loading and unloading crates containing life rafts. Does no one see them? Doesn't anyone wonder what they are for?

These inflatable objects are designed to save lives. "Setting people adrift is a flagrant violation of SAR regulations," explains Nora, "but what infuriates me the most is that it is, above all, an attack on seafaring ethics and instinct. The only thing worse than deliberately putting people in danger is pushing them out to sea."

ANOTHER LANDING

On the 5th of December 2023, 33 Afghan nationals landed in a dinghy on some rocks near the church of St George in the south-east of Lesbos. In the early afternoon, by chance, two journalists reached the forest where they were hiding before anyone else. One of them was the author of this article. The refugees had divided themselves into several small groups and spent 12 hours exposed to the elements, not smoking, keeping their voices down and their mobile phones on silent so as not to be discovered. The journalists, as well as taking an interest in their life stories and asking for permission to take photos, called 112 to inform the authorities. Three hours later, a police officer arrived and filed a report. Late in the evening, the refugees were taken by bus to the Kara Tepe camp, where they were searched.

The journalists lost contact with the Afghans, who stopped responding to their calls and messages. Weeks later, a third person told the reporters that the interrogation of the English-speaking refugees in that group had been particularly vigorous and focused on why there were two journalists in a forest a long way from the city. According to this third person, a police officer told the refugees that "if they didn't want trouble", they shouldn't associate with "those kinds of people".

The 10th of February and the 5th of December were just two days in a very long year. Since 2022, there has not been a week with two days in which no pushback was recorded. 33,607 people were rescued adrift in 2023. In 2022, that figure was 27,984. In the port of Mytilene, Lesbos, someone places a sticker next to a Hellenic Coast Guard boat that read: pushbacks are murder.

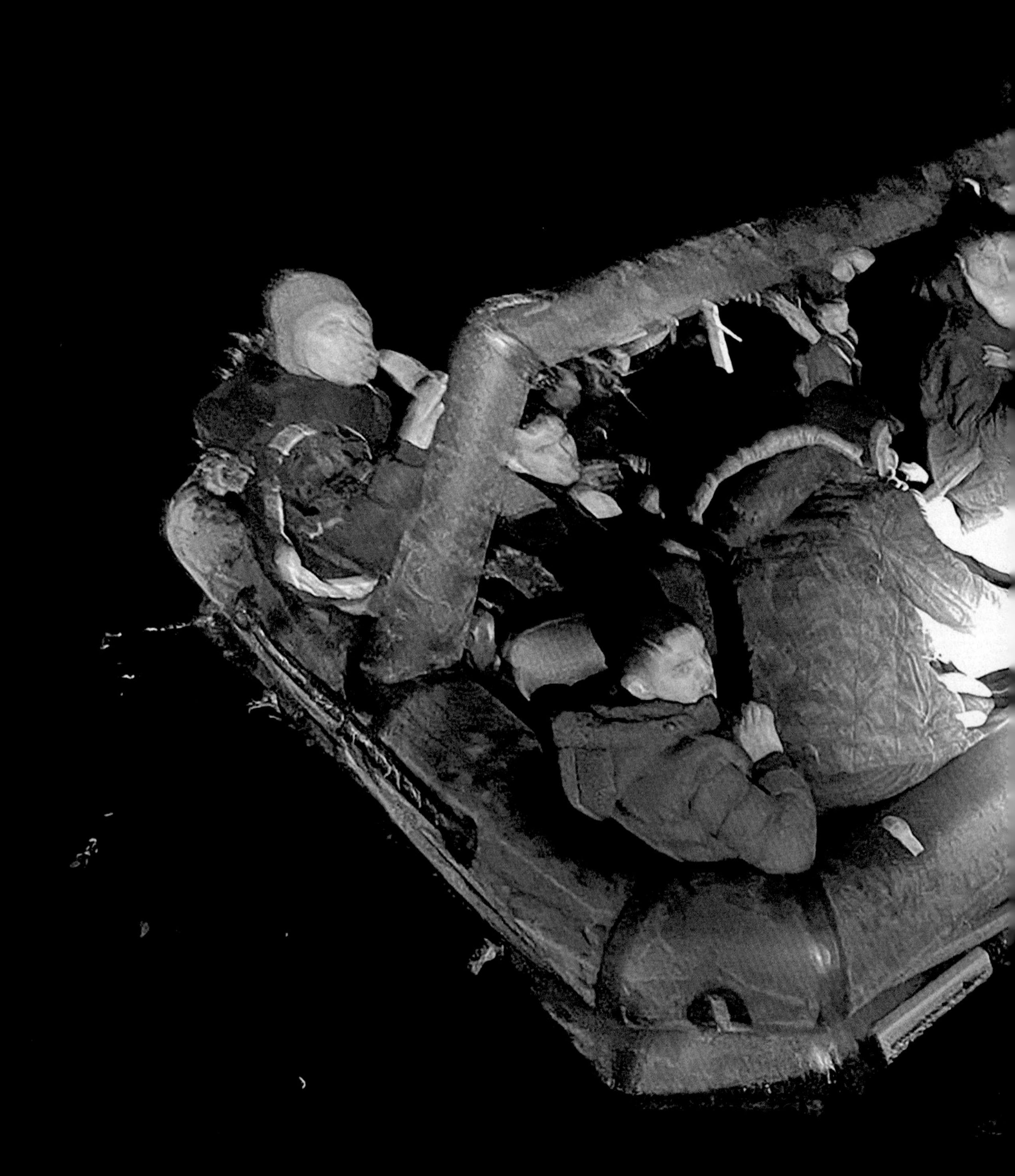

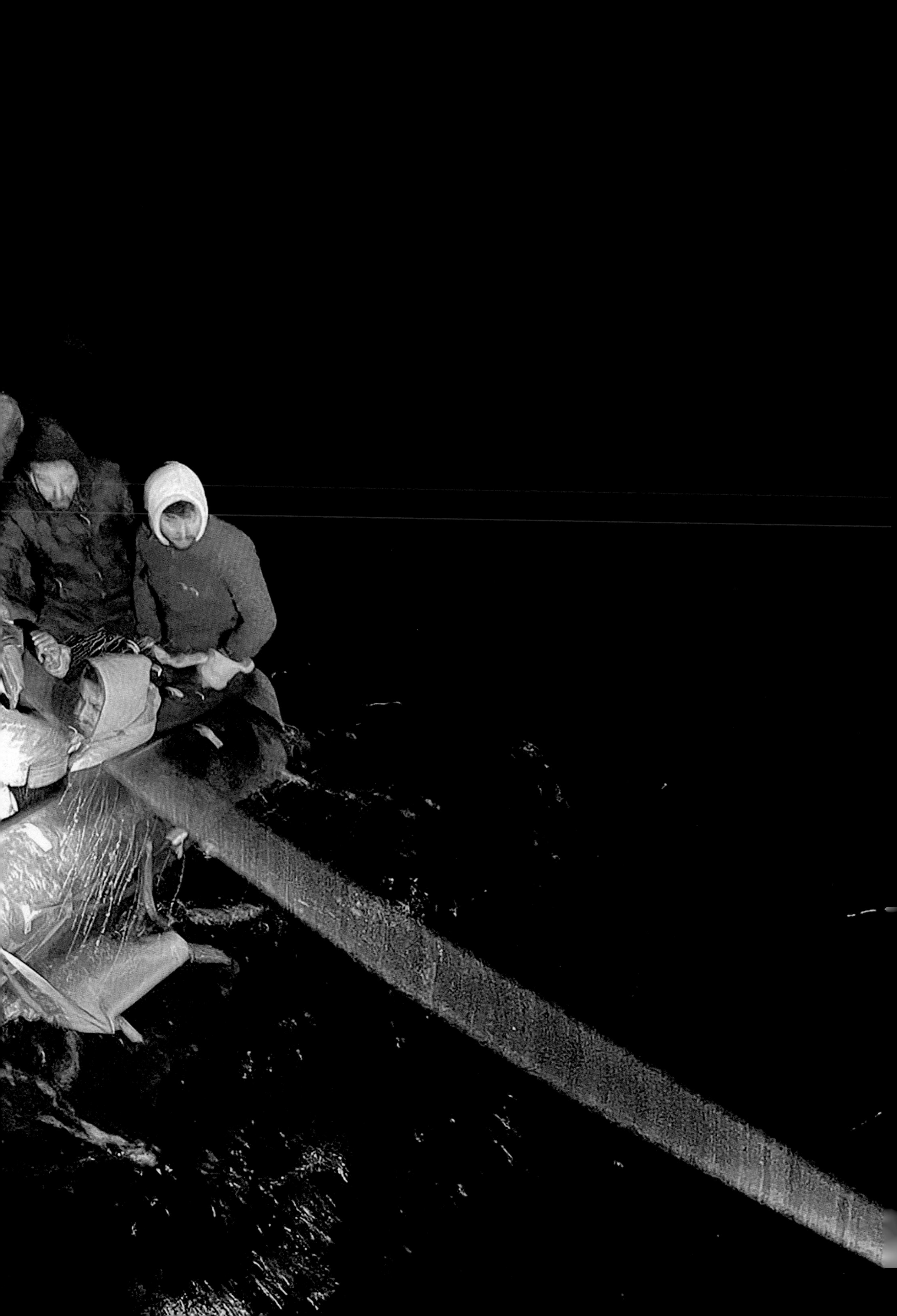

Hannah Meszaros Martin

TO BE KILLED IN THIS WAY. SOVEREIGN VIOLENCE AND THE BODY OF THE OUTLAW

The original image (above) was taken on DEA agent Steven Murphy's camera, presumably by another officer on the scene (2nd December, 1993).
The image that is most iconic was actually taken by the DEA agent and depicts the Colombian team of officers around the body. Image copyright: Abaca Press/ Alamy Stock Photo. *Narcos* chose to remake the image (below) with Steven Murphy in the frame. (*Narcos* Season 1, 2017) Image copyright: Netflix, Inc.

SCENE I

A shot in the light of day. Exposed on the tiled rooftops of Medellín, Pablo Escobar is gunned down, once, twice, then he falls, sprawled out on the broken tiles, still breathing as the hunters approach. The shooters gather around the body and someone takes out a pair of handcuffs, as if to gesture at the law. The voiceover narration spoken by the blond DEA agent is saying something about catching *him* finally, the chase ending or whatever, but he is interrupted when one of the policemen raises his gun and shoots Escobar in the head. The inane inner dialogue of the gringo ceases as they all start shooting at the body, already dead and disarmed in the light of day.

Everyone is cheering now. The scene cuts to archival footage and photographs of the actual kill. We learn that this is how it actually happened, on these ceramic rooftops, how the state killed the *ultimate outlaw*. The DEA agent lifts the dead, bloodied body by the shirt sleeve, avoiding touching the corpse. Lifting him just enough to expose his face as someone takes a snapshot. Then there is a cut to the original photograph. True to the original, the group composes itself around the prized kill. Like the traditional photographs of a hunter and his – because it is usually *his* – prey, the hunters position the dead body, the evidence of the kill, for the lens of the camera to capture. The scene ends and they cry out: *viva Colombia, viva Colombia, viva el Estado*. Long live Colombia. Long live the State.

Exiting the scene, the DEA agent climbs down from the rooftop. On the street below, he passes the paramilitary leaders, Don Berna (fittingly, he is standing next to a man in the military – the camera moves away as he leans over to whisper in his ear) and two of the Castaño brothers (there were three of them, but whatever) hovering in the background in the shadows of a tree.

This scene of death has been represented many times in many different forms of media, news, paintings, movies, and books. The one described above is from the Netflix series *Narcos*, which is how many people from the global North who had never been exposed to any of these representations saw this act of killing for the first time. The series, while it was severely lacking as a historical representation, played with something that, at one level, was meant to appeal to an international audience: the presentation of the outlaw as the subject whom we both love and hate; a fugitive whom we both want dead and want to escape all in the same moment.

The figure of the outlaw, however, does not only encompass human subjects. This is how we enter our second snapshot.

SCENE II

Many years later the scene changes. Another hunting party sets out to catch another outlaw. His name was Pepe. They say he was territorial, violent, invasive, a danger to the general public, and about 3.5 tons. Pepe was a hippopotamus. Pepe was also called a "fugitive," though a fugitive of what is a bit debatable. He had escaped the compound where his ancestors were brought in the early 1980s to the Hacienda Nápoles, Escobar's luxury-estate now turned tourist theme park.

Four shots. Two to the head and two to the heart. Pepe was killed in a clearing near his favorite grazing spot. The irony of the two killings was not lost on any reporter. How Escobar the drug lord and Pepe the hippo were killed in a strikingly similar way was widely commented on. One of the more disturbing connections is that in each case the man/beast-hunting party was coordinated by a kind-of foreign "killing expert." Pepe's death was coordinated by the CEO and the president of Autoelite, a corporation that represents the German auto company Porsche in Colombia, Federico and Christian Pfeil Schneider. In the case of Escobar there was of course the gringo DEA agent, Steven Murphy.

The head of the slain animal became part of the CEO's private collection. A trophy-kill *par excellence*, the ultimate outlaw's outlaw hippo now sits in the luxury auto company CEO's collection of dead animals.

The news tipped into the international sphere. In fact, the most infamous drug lord's rogue hippos consistently attract global newsrooms in a country where much goes unreported. The *New York Times* wrote: "Even in Colombia, a country known for its paramilitary death squads, this hunting party stood out: more than a dozen soldiers from a Colombian Army battalion, two Porsche salesmen armed with long-range rifles, their assistant, and a taxidermist." I am not sure the *New York Times* fully appreciated the irony to be found in the comparison between a paramilitary death-squad and a hunting party led by multinational executives, themselves protected by the Colombian army.

The snapshot of the hunting party, presumably taken on a soldier's cellphone, was leaked to the press and caused such a public outrage that the other two hippos who were also fugitives of the state – Pepe's mate Matilda and their offspring, simply called "Hip" – were spared the same fate.

In the image, the hunting party encircles the dead hippo. His wet skin glistens in the light of the flash. The soldiers pose with their guns. Most look towards the camera. Some are looking at the hippo. Three men reach out and place their hands – almost gently – on the dead body. Touching the wild animal, now tamed and dead, can be read as an act of final dominance over nature. The gesture transmits a message: *We won, we killed the beast*. The light touch of the men on the wet skin of the hippo confirms this dominance for the camera and us as the audience. (see fig.1)

A "snapshot" is in fact originally a hunting term, meaning to "shoot from the hip." The term signified a combined act of movement and sight: the hunter walks with the gun barrel disengaged, then sees the sudden appearance of prey, "snaps" to engage the weapon, and shoots ("shot") often from the hip as there is not enough time to bring the gunsight up to one's eye. Snapshot was applied to photography in the late 19th century, a period during which the act of hunting and image-making were being thought together.[1] There was even the invention of "camera hunting," which came about in the US to describe the act of going out into "Nature" to look for and photograph different forms of wildlife. The inventors of the term argued that this activity was in fact a kind of hunting, involving the same forms of knowledge and actions that went into stalking your prey, though instead of being armed with a gun, you are armed with a camera. In "camera hunting," a "trophy kill" is not a dead animal

fig.1 Author unknown, 16th June, 2009. The image created such a scandal that the photographer did not come forward.

hanging on the wall, but rather the image itself.[2] Hunting snapshots, which depict the hunters and their prey, however, pre-date camera hunting. In this practice, the corpse and the photograph merge as the animal-as-trophy and the image-as-trophy become one and the same.

When looking at the two trophy images side-by-side – the body of Escobar and the body of Pepe – photography, hunting, and death, which produced the concept of the snapshot, come together to tell another story. This story is one of sovereign and masculine violence, the outlaw and the act of killing with impunity.

Representations of killing animals and hunting parties are some of the earliest works of art. The "Assyrian Lion Hunts," a series of carved stone reliefs that now line a hallway of the British Museum in London, are a part of this canon. They are early examples of realist representations of the pain and suffering of animals. The slabs of stone, like many objects in the colonial museum, were taken from what is now modern-day Iraq.

In the reliefs, we see the lions in varying stages of dying. The narrative of their death unfolds along the wall, embedded in the stone. The king's hunting party releases the lions from their captivity into an arena – a controlled setting for the hunt. The chase begins. Then each lion is killed as the hunters cast their spears from their royal chariots. (see fig.2)

In ancient Assyria, lions were also considered a menace to the general public – killing livestock and interfering with daily life and economies; an obstruction to "civilized" modes of being. The king was meant to demonstrate that he could control their presence, even eliminating them from his domain. The Assyrian royal seal depicts a king slaying a lion. Killing the animal – both in the wild and in the spectacle of the arena – became essential acts of the sovereign and the construction of his sovereignty: the king establishing his power through his dominance over nature, his ability to capture and kill it. The stone reliefs are a display of ultimate sovereignty. Sovereignty enacted through the killing of "the wild" through slaying a being considered to be the most powerful in that realm.

One image stands out in the series, depicting a dying lioness. She has been shot with arrows in the back; the nerves cut; she drags her legs in agony over the ground. Her face screams. It is possible, in what was supposed to be a celebration of the power to rule over the natural world, that the artist achieved the opposite: a hyper-realistic rendition of the lions' suffering, of their desperation. In the reliefs, the cold, almost person-less expression of the hunter is held in stark contrast to the detailed depiction of sheer emotion and pain in the face of the animal. In this attention to detail, the viewer's sympathy goes to the lion. As we watch the sovereign exert his power to kill the creatures with impunity, our eyes are directed by the artist towards the dying beast, wishing she could escape.[3]

When nature and nonhumans are criminalized and fall into the realm of the outlaw, they are posited not as passive beings or victims of a destructive and violent war, but rather as active agents, who themselves can be violent and destructive, a threat to society-at-large. Their identification as "outlaws" justifies their ultimate destruction; their death falls within the realm of the law, within the sovereign's right to kill.

fig.2 The dying lioness from the Assyrian Lion Hunts. Panel from the North Palace of Ashurbanipal, from northern Iraq, 645-635 BC. The British Museum, London. Image: Robert Martin.

FINAL SCENE

In order to understand these two snapshots it is necessary to go back to the legal and ideological origins of the term "outlaw."

The concept has been traced to Roman law, to the *Homo Sacer*, or the "sacred man" who cannot be sacrificed yet can be killed with impunity.[4] This figure represented, in a sense, the most extreme form of exile. An exile that forced one to leave not just the particular city that happened to be one's home, but rather the city as such, all cities, the city as symbol of civilization, culture, and society – the human realm. Once expelled, one was considered to be *outside the law*, and therefore outside the law's protection. Most crucially, being *outside* human society was perceived as being somehow *against* it; thus, the figure of the outlaw was seen to be "an opponent of the city and its people."[5] The opponent of the *city* was then against society, and therefore, against the State. Here, a line is drawn between what is thought of as "civilization" and what is considered to be "the rural" and "the wild."

German legal scholars of the 19th and 20th centuries cite the word "warg," meaning werewolf, as the ancient Germanic legal term for *outlaw*.[6] "Warg, they said, meant 'wolf' because the outlaw, like the wolf, lived in the forest and might be killed with impunity by anyone."[7] This "magico-legal pronouncement" can also be found in Old Norse Icelandic law, ancient legal Hittite texts as well as continental Germanic law. In Anglo-Norman law the outlaw was he who bore a wolf's head.

The law's transfiguration of the human subject into something *less than human* meant that the outlaw could be killed with impunity. His body, now joined with that of "the beast," was considered to be outside the protection of the law. In this way, the outlaw also came to define the borders of the human subject. However, there is a paradox that resides within this notion of the outlaw, because while being cast out-of-law, the subject can still be punished by it.

Giorgio Agamben uses the figure of the *Homo Sacer*, which he argues is the representation of bare life, the exception that is derived from exclusion, to establish the preconditions of sovereignty. For him, it is significant that the *Homo Sacer* was related – "a brother" he says – to the figure of the werewolf (a being that blurs the distinction between the human and the nonhuman) and not just an animal.

Agamben draws out several paradoxes underlying the subject of the *Homo Sacer*/werewolf/outlaw, themselves reflective of paradoxes contained within State sovereignty. Both the sovereign and the *Homo Sacer* share the same paradoxical condition of being both outside and inside the law.[8] The sovereign who both establishes the law and has the power to suspend it (thereby creating the state of exception) is itself outside the law (and above it). Outlawed life-forms inhabit the same contradiction, since "what is excluded in the exception maintains itself in relation to the rule in the form of the rule's suspension."[9] According to this logic, outlaw as a term is an oxymoron, as there is in fact no being that is "out-of-law."

Pablo Escobar imported the original four hippopotamuses from the US (of course it was the US) sometime in the early 1980s. He also brought giraffes, kangaroos and even a rhinoceros into the country; an act that can also be read as his own enactment of a kind of sovereignty, circumventing the laws of the state while also establishing a mastery of the "wild" by forming his own zoo. Though, it is possible that he didn't envision his sovereign act as being quite so transformative environmentally as it has become in recent decades.

Pepe escaped with his mate and their baby in 2006. It wasn't until June of 2009 that he was found and killed. The escaped hippos are now many more in number; an estimated 170 hippos roaming wild in the Magdalena river basin. Concerns over their impacts for the ecosystems in Colombia have only grown since Pepe was killed.

In March 2022, the Ministry of the Environment declared the hippo an invasive species in Colombia. As animal rights activists are opposed to more killing, the government's solution – for now – is a mass sterilization combined with bringing the animals to sanctuaries in different countries.

The descendants of Escobar's original four are now unfortunately (for them) referred to as 'cocaine hippos'. Cocaine is the alkaloid derivative of the coca plant, the substance which helped Escobar to construct the forms of sovereignty that made the importation of the hippo possible in the first place (the authors of the term were either thinking of this or the film *Cocaine Bear*). Coca is another outlawed being that can be killed with impunity.[10] The enforced eradication of the plant with the herbicide glyphosate is an example of how in the long durée of the Colombian war, the concept of the outlaw encompasses a full-spectrum of different beings, both human and non-human, and has shaped the ways in which violence has been conducted. The coca leaf, posited as the enemy of the state, is subject to a mass, legalized, and enforced eradication.

These outlawed specters of the state, the plants, animals, and the humans who live by their side, the hippo who escapes a drug lord's pleasure palace, the body(ies) of the guerrilla, living not only in the forest but also within the city walls, are the ones who can be hunted down and killed with impunity. The construct of the outlaw has produced a border that has defined the human subject, the sovereign, and who/what it is permissible to kill or let die.[11] Who is mourned and who is buried in a shallow grave along the Magdalena River, whose head is hung on a CEO's wall filled with the dead of the world.

1 Metz, Gary. 1980. History of Photography Course, International Center of Photography, New York
2 See Brower, Mathew. 2011. *Developing animals: wildlife and early American photography*. Minneapolis: University of Minnesota Press
3 Thanks to conversations with my father, Robert Martin and his work on the William E. Parker lectures on the Mimetic Tradition, Visual Studies Workshop, Rochester, New York, 1977. (Lectures>Visual Studies Workshop 1977> lecture #4A) found at: http://williameparker.com
4 Agamben, Giorgio. 1998. *Homo Sacer: sovereign power and bare life*. Stanford: Stanford UniversityPress
5 Heller-Roazen, Daniel. 2009. *The enemy of all: piracy and the law of nations*. New York: Zone, p. 101
6 See for example Gerstein, Mary R. 1974. "Germanic *warg*: the outlaw as werwolf." In *Myth in Indo-European Antiquity*, edited by Gerald James Larson, C. Scott Littleton and Jaan Puhvel, p. 131. Berkeley: University of California Press
7 Gerstein, ibid., p. 133-134
8 "I, the sovereign, who am outside the law, declare that there is nothing outside the law." Agamben, Giorgio. 1988. *Homo Sacer: Sovereign Power and Bare Life*. Agamben., p. 16. Stanford University Press
9 Ibid., p. 18
10 Martin, H. J. M. 2019. "The outlawed earth: spectrums of violence, the visible and the politics of *Violencia Ambiental*." PhD diss., Goldsmiths College, University of London
11 The counterpoint between to kill and to let die comes from Foucault. See: Foucault, Michel. 2002. *Society must be defended: lectures at the College De France*, 1975-76. Translated by David Macey, edited by Mauro Bertani and Alessandro Fontana. New York: Picador, p. 241.

A version of this piece was first published in Spanish in: https://ediciones.uniandes.edu.co/library/publication/belicopedia.

THE COAL MINE

"7 km from the frontline and 1 km underground, the men and women of the Pokrovsk coal mine continue to work even though the Russian military is slowly advancing in their direction. Since the start of the full-scale invasion of Ukraine in 2022, over half of the workforce in this mine has quit to join the Ukrainian military. Despite the smaller workforce, work continues as usual below ground as the mining industry is vital to the war effort by providing fuel and raw materials to the military. Just weeks before my visit it was struck by a Russian artillery strike, which resulted in one person being killed and many buildings above ground being badly damaged. However, the threat of violence does not deter the workforce. Every day, hundreds of workers still show up despite the distant boom of artillery. I arrive at the mine as a shift change is taking place, men completely black with coal dust exit a lift, the whites of their eyes and teeth presenting a stark contrast compared to the rest of their bodies. Most stay silent as they file past me and clean themselves before going home, a nod of recognition or a slap on the back as a bus load of spotless miners arrive for the next 12-hour shift."

Conall Kearney (Cocobongo666)

RS OF DONBAS

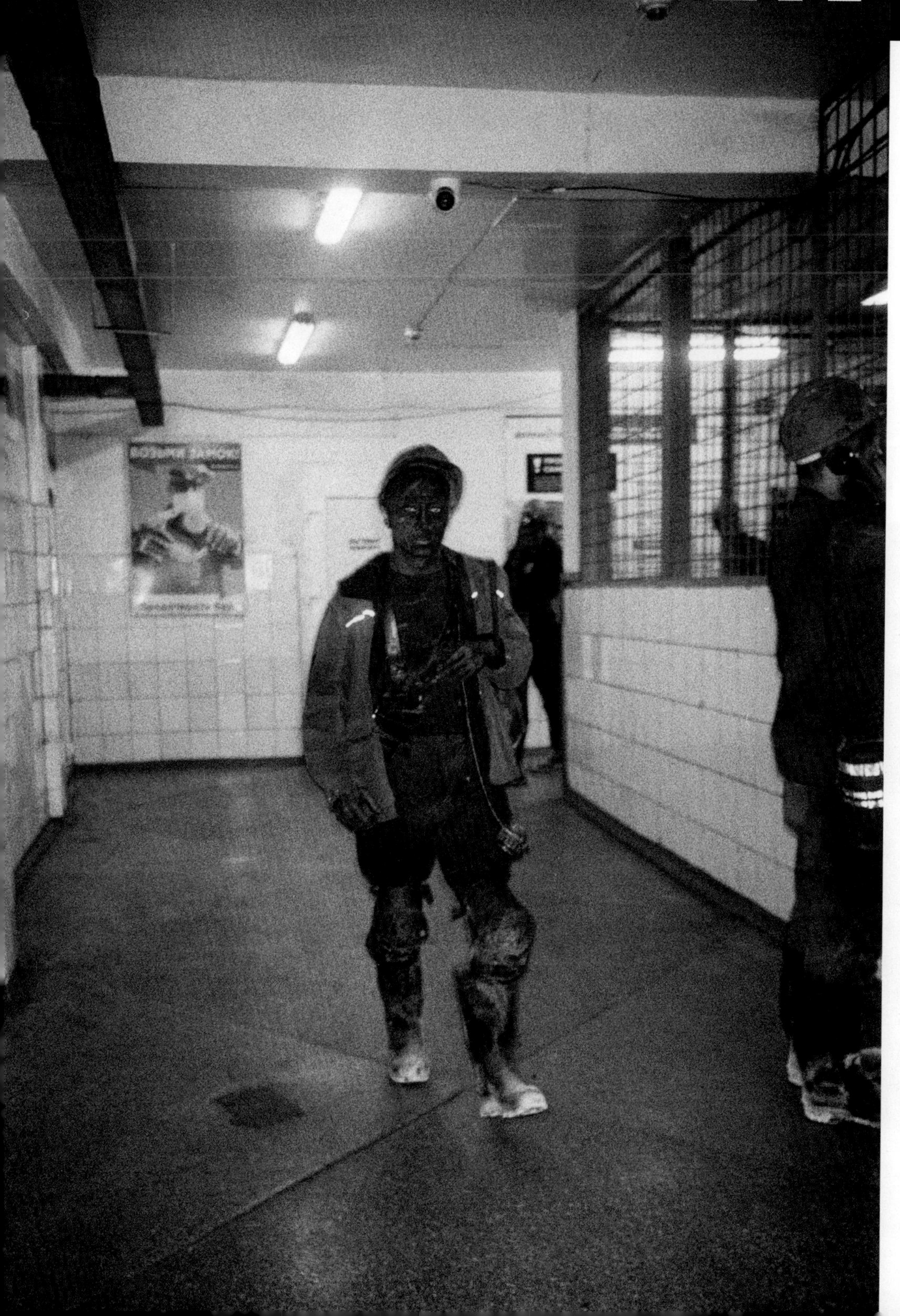

B
2
уч-к УКТ-9

Горный диспетчер
47-306
Медпункт
47-303
Диспетчер по транспорту
47-366
Коммутатор
2

Місце
зупинки
автобусів

СПАСИ И СОХРАНИ

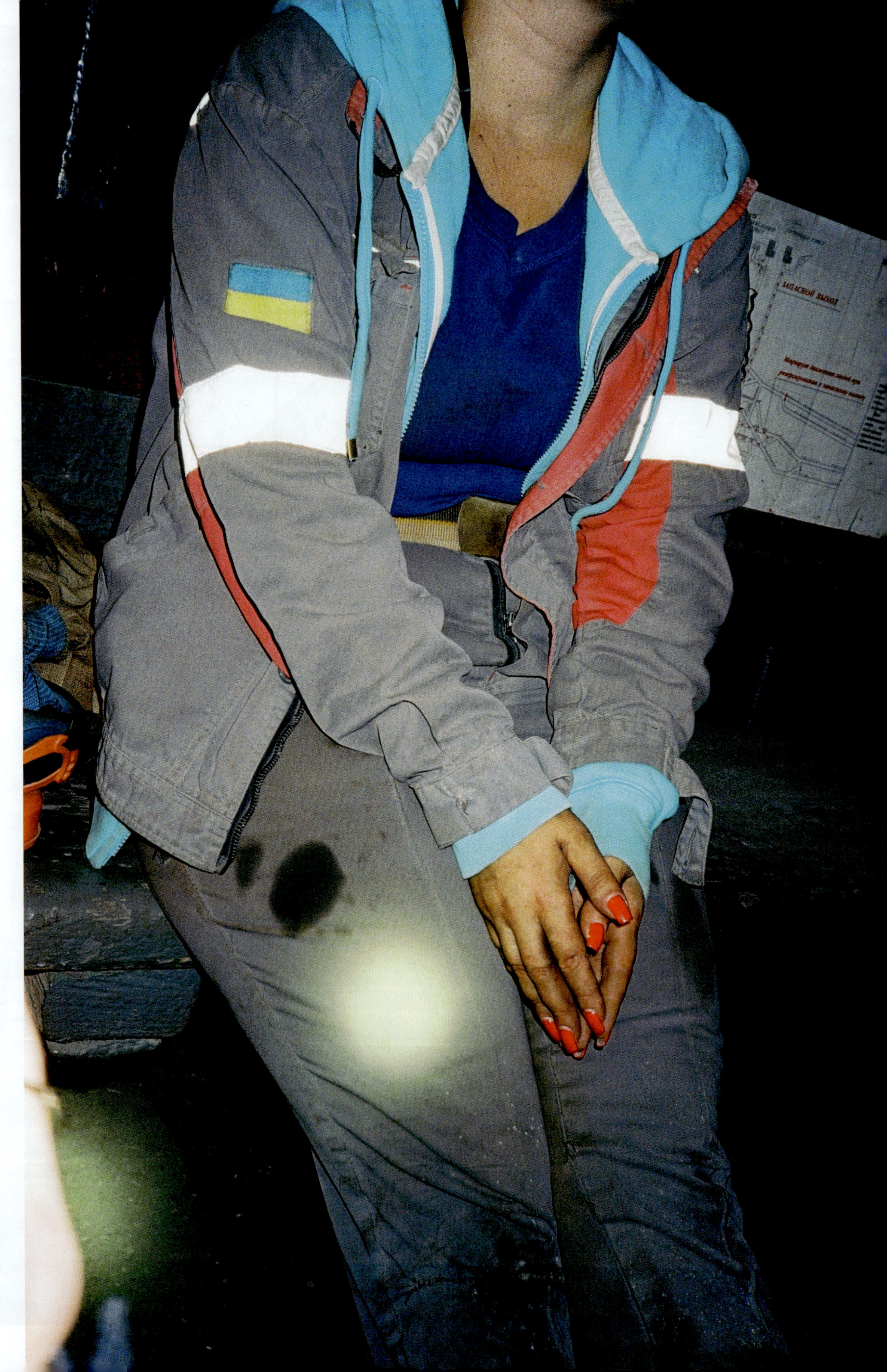
ЗАПАСНОЙ ВЫХОД

801-1000
1001-1200
601-800

table."[4] This is why I like to think that *rikimbili* names, above all, a creole power of association. The *rikimbili*—at the level of the idea—has as much associative power and creative potential as the mind of a *conspiranoid* individual.

There is no difference between the two states of a *rikimbili*: assembled and disassembled. The same force that combines its parts separates them. The mosaic law that joins the mechanical fragments is the same law that pulls them apart. In a context of so much need, where direct sale and purchase operate as an immediate economic spillway, it's to be expected that an assembled *rikimbili* would figure only as the *tactical display*—a provisional one—that seeks to catch the eye of a potential buyer. Nevertheless, the assembled *rikimbili* is a promise, a work in progress, something that cannot be finished—and if completed, could not be a *rikimbili*.

Sometimes, *rikimbilis* can't be seen. They are first built as messages on WhatsApp, or as posts on Facebook. The post as a film editing table. You write what you have, and the comments operate like addition or subtraction processes in the production of your *rikimbili*. Some people criticize you or offer you solutions; others make offers to buy or sell. The collection of texts is also an assembly; it's a *rikimbili*. For this reason, it's common for many people to refer to their *rikimbilis* as projects.[5] "Hi, this is my project, don't criticize it too much." That's the first line of a post that recurs day after day, week after week. *Rikimbilism* as a hobby. On the one hand, as we've already seen, the *rikimbili* is associated with need. Its greatest presence and relevance coincided with the Special Period in the Time of Peace. The fuel shortage after the reduction of the economic relations with the USSR demanded of individuals and families that they find alternative means of transportation, both for passengers and cargo. If it is true that the term was used in cities only for the purpose of naming bicycles with motors, then it is just as true that it was used, and has been since then, in rural areas to name all types of home-made vehicles. But, on the other hand, Cuban *rikimbilians* now form a club in which they refer to their devices as projects and expect to hear the opinions of their colleagues in the same way that occurs in the forums for karting and model airplanes.

In the last few weeks, news and a publication by the regime has been unsettling the *rikimbilian* forums. In the *Gaceta Oficial N. 63 Extraordinaria* from July 20th, 2021, the regime put out Resolution Number 200, through which the government is effecting a "process of homologation of motor vehicles, trailers, semi-trailers, assembled with parts and pieces." It's surprising that the editors of the *Gaceta Oficial* employed the term *riquimbili*. The newspapers from the rural areas say that on August 5th, they will begin the process, and committees will be placed in every region to review and approve the vehicles. In Article 8.1 of the Resolution, it states: "The Committee, regarding those vehicles declared Apt, will denominate them Vehicle Assembled from Parts, abbreviated VAP, and should it resemble an existing brand, then to its name will be added the denomination of that brand." With the proposal of the VAP, the state joins the effort to discover new terms that could bring order to the revolt that has been shaking up Cuba's material culture for several decades now. Following the normative principle of the state, I predict that "VAP" will also be useful in naming *Viviendas* [Housing] Assembled from Parts. In the pictures of *rikimbilis*, one can see, as I've already said, parts of homes made by the same people that make the *rikimbilis*. Additionally, as I've already explained, the pieces become confused with the designs and fragments of the floor tiles. If VAP is *rikimbili*, *rikimbili* is *Architecture of necessity*.[6]

The news about the new process of homologation prompted enormous activity on the forums dedicated to these necessities. The state expects the *rikimbilis* to comply with technical, legal, and formal demands that are difficult to satisfy. Frankly speaking, amnesty was expected. For this reason, there are many pessimistic comments on the forums of Facebook and WhatsApp that attribute a controlling and discriminatory role to Resolution Number 200, more so than a conciliatory and inclusive one. On the one hand we have: technical automotive norms; formal and structural demands; and the existence of documentation of ownership for each part used in the construction of a *rikimbili* (purchase receipts or sworn testimonies that the piece was not stolen from the state or an individual). On the other hand we have a torrent of unclassifiable, unfinished, improvised devices, pieces and parts that are overflowing, I would say. The only thing all of these objects share is that they exist to satisfy the need for transportation that has not been met by the state's centralized economy. It may be that the *rikimbili* does not fit the regulatory framework of the state, but it has covered the empty space left by the state in its incapacity to solve the severe transportation problem that afflicts the island. The *rikimbili* has always filled an empty space; that's what it's about. The *rikimbili* is a meta-placeholder. Many provisional objects created by Cubans to confront the economic crisis qualify for that title. The *rikimbili* is a substitute, a vicarious object that temporarily holds the place created in the culture by another object, now absent.

I'm going to go ahead now and sneak in—as if I were putting a Lombardini irrigation motor on the frame of a creole bicycle—the first notes of an ode: *Rikimbili* as *placeholder*. This term used to be employed in graphic design to name the black rectangles that occupied, in the pre-press archives, the areas destined for illustrations and photographs. Other terms close to placeholder in different contexts: proxy, vicar, substitute, surrogate, succedaneum, and ersatz. The Pope, as we know, is the vicar of Rome, something like Jesus Christ's placeholder on Earth. It's precisely in the power structure that this tactical placeholder role survives. I wonder: What political potentialities reside in the placeholder image? When it temporarily occupies a space, be it a graphical surface, a physical space, or a discourse—what political possibilities does the image enable at its insertion? Undoubtedly, the placeholder is that tactical object that, upon its insertion, contaminates, corrupts, empowers, amplifies, or interrogates the space it comes to occupy. Isn't that what the Pope does? Now I am seized by doubt: is the "Popemobile" a *rikimbili*?

We know how the *rikimbili* impacts the city, at the level of sound for example. In Havana, you don't see any *rikimbilis,* but you hear them as they furtively circulate on the backstreets. The sound is the same as the one provoked by an individual who charges toward you, a running chainsaw in his hands, and then keeps going past you until the sound disappears. But in what other way does the *rikimbili* challenge our lives? What critical look at design does this object propose? How does it challenge the aesthetic, utilitarian, authorial and consumer notions entrenched in culture by the

1 Rikimbili. Bicycle propelled by a fumigation device engine, Havana. Archive Technological Disobedience.Photo E. Oroza, 2005
2 Rikimbili. Bicycle propelled by a military tank engine. Havana. Research image from Archive Technological Disobedience.Photo E. Oroza, 2005
3 Rikimbili. Bicycle propelled by a water pump engine. Havana. Research image from Archive Technological Disobedience.Photo E. Oroza, 2005

4 Rikimbili. Bicycle propelled by a hand saw engine, Havana. Archive Technological Disobedience. Photo E. Oroza, 2005.

5, 6 Tactical placeholder. Children's playground, at the Havana Zoo, repaired with inflatable toys that are removed from the structures every day. Research image from Archive Technological Disobedience.Photo E Oroza, 2017.

market? Thinking about the *rikimbili* from design is already corrosive to certain strata based on the idea that design as a discipline should only be practiced by professionals. What space does this intruder make for new questions, ideas, and devices? What does this *object of necessity* propose in terms of production? Thinking of the *rikimbili* as a placeholder grants us a wider look at it and at its context of insertion. For the moment, we've realized its capacity to expose the rigid framework being used to try to trap it. The *rikimbili* as a placeholder is, at the same time, both an indicator (index) of its placeholder function and an indicator (index, deictic) of the dimensions or the qualities of the absent, of that which has allowed it, by some trace of similarity, to occupy its place. The placeholder is a photo of the "frame," and the latter frames what is framing it: because of its need to match up, it ends up describing the context into which it is inserted. Perhaps we can't answer even the first of the questions in this paragraph, but we can accept the *rikimbili* as a document and as a precipitate of current Cuban society. To think of the *rikimbili* as an archive. That's another trip.

EPILOGUE I (CARA DE PALO)

"Cara de palo" (literal translation: wooden face) is another Cuban term for automobiles created or altered by individuals with parts and pieces from other automobiles. The idea that cars have faces is as universal as automobiles and as universal as the media and materials where cars are depicted talking or with facial expressions. This interpretation, a result of the pareidolia phenomenon, is caused by the configuration of the front of cars, specifically the relationship between the headlights (eyes), the radiator and hood ornament (nose), and the front bumper (mouth). "Cara de palo" can be read, in this sense, as a strange, ungraceful, stiff face with a comical expression. It can also be used to name a face that is the result of an improvised creation, made with what is found, and not as the result of a design process. In slang, and beyond the production of cars, "Cara de palo" (like "cara dura") is a term that refers to people who are not ashamed of public scorn and who seek at all costs their own benefit and above the established order. A "wooden face" is an entity that defies order, in this case traffic laws and urban order.

EPILOGUE II (PLATELESS CAR PEOPLE'S MOVEMENT)

On Friday, November 10th, 2023, in an appearance on Cuban television, the current head of the national registry of vehicles and licenses declared the homologation process terminated. The joint response from the thousands of affected people, who were unable to register their *rikimbilis*, was not long in coming. On November 20th, a new Facebook group, self-titled "Movimiento Social Los Sin Chapa" (Plateless Car People's Movement), addressed an open letter to the government. In it they demanded the extension of the homologation process while listing the irregularities they have suffered, which, according to them, caused the delay of registrations in all provinces. Self-defined as a social movement (later changed on the group's page as a movement of social interaction) they declare the following rules for belonging to the group: forbidden to talk about politics; forbidden to offend any comrade; forbidden to echo unofficial news; forbidden to publish sales; forbidden to discuss any topic outside the official group; forbidden to use the group to call for any kind of demonstrations.

The last rule shocked me. I had imagined a gigantic troop of vehicles armed with parts and pieces traveling through all the streets of the country in the direction of the capital to gather in front of the Ministry of Transportation to demand their rights. I imagined this as a great parade of parts and pieces moving from east to west. If the starting of the engines for that protest should respond to a need for social justice, very soon, that march of the plateless car people would become a huge VAP parade, a conga of *rikimbilis*, a spectacle of disobedient design. If it were made possible, we would see thousands of Lada, Peugeot, and Hyundai emblems on the fronts of *rikimbilis*, but no vehicle looking remotely like a Lada, Peugeot, or Hyundai. Only the sound of the engines would justify the use of these emblems. And if they were organized by emblems and all those with Lada engines were gathered in one block, we would not find among them two vehicles alike. Even if they share the same type of engine and perhaps the differential, all the bodies and structures would be different. It is possible that some typologies stand out, in the same way that the *bicitaxis* of the province of Camagüey, although very diverse among them, are typologically different from the *bicitaxis* of the province of Matanzas. The regional typological distinctions depend on vernacular knowledge, local needs and uses. It is not the same to intend a *rikimbili* for agricultural areas as for urban use. Sometimes it is a technical inventor who creates a trend. For example, if someone finds a way to adapt a Moskvitch gearbox to a Lombardini irrigation engine, he will make it easier for many in his area to copy him. Resources available by region also inform typologies. Other resources have a national presence. Perhaps for this reason in this hypothetical VAP parade we would notice the use of thousands of meters of red, yellow, green, and blue plastic tarps, making up the bodies of the motorized tricycles. Consequently, and perhaps out of a need for formal integration, we would discover that *rikimbileros* from all over the country have used paints in those same colors to cover the rest of the body of their *rikimbilis*.

One of the surprises of the parade would be to see all these vehicles driving on the main roads. It would make no sense to hide along interior streets. Therefore, the characteristic sound that many times announces their passing through the neighborhoods will now correspond to the presence of these vehicles on the central roads. The highest note of this automotive sound show will be produced by a horde of self-declared "fanáticos del rodillo" (transmission roller fans). *Rikimbilis* identified as "motores por rodillo" represent in this group the oldest typological caste, they are the originals, they would say. They are bicycles to which a motor from a saw, or from a fumigation device or a water pump has been added. The transmission of the movement of the motor to the external face of the rear wheel is carried out by means of the piece that they call "rodillo." This is an essential object in the *rikimbili* culture. There are other important elements that allow the connection of the motor to the bike and secure the structure, but the part that produces the real coupling and functionality is the direct transmission roller. It is a longitudinally grooved cylinder. Its diameter is around five and a half centimeters, and the length up to twelve centimeters, but the variety is enormous. Many have been fabricated from the end of transmission rods from cars such as Ladas, while others have been built with steel pipes machined on metal lathes. The form of coupling to the engine varies according to the engine. Many are strictly tubular; others have a base plate for connection. It is quite possible that when this demonstration occurs these hordes of *fans al rodillo* will make the journey to the capital competing. And not only in speed, they will also compete for the best *tuning*, and even the best *beef* (*tiraderas*, challenging, boasts, and statements inscribed on the bikes). I wonder if these public messages will serve as a prologue to other messages, to those where the participants of this protest/parade claim their civil rights.

1 *Rikimbili* is the term used in Cuba, since the 90s, to name the vehicle made by adding a gas motor to a bicycle. Today the term includes all vehicles built from various parts. I write the word *rikimbili* with a "k" because it is one of the common forms, and because that letter, as well as the "y," for a few decades now, have been used repeatedly in the creation of new names for people on the island. Both letters have an important role in the new creole onomastics

2 Other motors brought into the country over the last few decades and mentioned frequently in the *rikimbilian* forums are: Hero Gizmo Honda, Hero Honda Panther, Piaggio, Champion, Wiper, UD15, Micuni AX100, Isuzu, Yanmar, and Ruggerini

3 I am thinking of this line by Jorge Luis Borges: "Philosophies are nothing more than a coordination of words." Borges, Jorge Luis. 1932. *Avatares de la tortuga. Obras Completas*, vol. 3. Sudamericana

4 Lautréamont, Conde de. 2014. *Obras completas. Canto sexto*, p. 236. Buenos Aires: Editorial Argonauta

5 On August 19th, 2021, user Ale Santos published, in "*Rikimbilis de Cuba Compra y Ventas*," photos of his device and wrote: "Hi, group! Here you can see my project, still unfinished. A little motor from a Sthil 441 chainsaw, a 70 cc 50 mm piston, centrifugal clutch, and it has 5.7 cv. I'm open to all types of criticism. Greetings." The next day, user Leo Merlin uploaded two photos of his *rikimbili* and wrote: "My little project, suggestions and critiques are welcome." A third user announced: "Good evening group, I'm selling this unfinished project, Lombardini motor (86 mm), 3-speed transmission with reverse, chain differential, all factory-made from a scooter, factory-made front, new tires, non-pneumatic tires (13" rim). It's in Matanzas."

6 www.architectureofnecessity.com

7

7 Research image from Archive Architecture of necessity. Photo E Oroza, 2012.

FUNERARY TECHNOLOGY AS A WEAPON OF WAR

Hibai Arbide

One of the biggest secrets of the Ukrainian war is the number of wounded and, above all, the number of dead. Since the beginning of the Russian invasion in February 2022, both sides have been hiding the figures for their own casualties while publishing exaggerated estimates for the opposing side. They do this to avoid demoralising their population and to prevent the enemy from having an accurate picture of the outcome of their attacks. Thus, only details of civilian casualties are published. Secrecy is not unique to this conflict. Ever since public opinion played a key role in ending the Vietnam War, modern wars have been fought with less and less transparency and increasing attempts to control the information to which journalists have access.

At the same time, since the late 19th century and particularly during the 20th century, Western armies have been paying homage to the "unknown soldier". Since Denmark erected the Landsoldaten (infantry soldier) monument in the First Prusso-Danish War, many European and American states have erected cenotaphs dedicated to a generic soldier rather than a specific one. After World War I, the United Kingdom buried an anonymous combatant in Westminster Abbey on behalf of all the armies of the British Empire. A year later, in 1921, France buried an unidentified infantry soldier under the Arc de Triomphe in Paris in the world's most famous monument to an unknown soldier. Subsequently, 40 other states adopted this form of commemoration.

But there are regions in the world where neither secrecy nor anonymous tributes come into play. Indeed, there are conflicts in which armed actors view their casualties not only as something not to hide but as information they strive to propagate by all means. The epitome of this is Hezbollah, which not only makes no effort to hide how many of its members die in combat but, on the contrary, turns their funerals and graves into proof of their commitment. One example of this are the dedicated Telegram channels: since the beginning of the current phase of the war in Gaza, which soon spread to southern Lebanon, the broadcasting groups detail every day the number of dead, the origin of their families, whether they have relatives who have fallen before, the place of combat where they lost their lives, and so on. Moreover, at the end of each day, these details are added to a final daily tally in which the names, origins and numbers of the campaign's dead are recalled under the epilogue "martyred in the line of duty on the path to Jerusalem". At the time of writing, 161 fighters had fallen.

One of the first to fall, along with three of his comrades on the 9th of October 2023, was Mohammad Hassan Mansour. He came from Mashghara, a small village in the Beqaa valley. Mohammad was very young and had just become a father. Despite this, when his father heard that he had died, he said, "God help the children of Palestine. You were my son, Mohammad; now you are the son of Hezbollah; now you are the martyr Mohammad Hassan Mansour. Thank you, God, for this honour." Immediately afterwards, in front of everyone present, he embraced his other son and proclaimed, "Now it is your turn or mine; we will join Mohammad."

The Lebanese armed party (literally, "The Party of God") is often portrayed as a puppet of Iran; a mere executor of Tehran's plans. Yet, although Iran has been its financier and main supporter since its founding in 1982, Hezbollah is already a regional actor in its own right, with its own autonomous agenda. While it has never diminished its ties with the Ayatollahs' regime, Hassan Nasrallah's group has demonstrated a strategic capacity and, above all, a nationalist political leadership in Lebanon that has made it much more than just a proxy of Iran. This leadership relies on two factors: its enormous support in the Shia community (which, of the 18 recognised faiths in Lebanon, has grown the most in recent decades to become the most dominant) and its military might. Hezbollah is probably the most powerful non-state actor in the world in military terms, having won two victories over Israel, in 2000 and 2006, and being an active participant in the Syrian war, which, although unpopular among its grassroots supporters, ultimately served to furnish it with tanks, medium-range missiles and air and naval forces that it didn't have before. In any case, the point to understand is that the Party of God is a complex movement that cannot be interpreted simplistically. In this text, we will limit our focus to one of its most distinctive aspects: its funerary technology.

HEZBOLLAH'S MAUSOLEUMS

The southern suburbs of Beirut, comprising several municipalities, are collectively known as Dahieh. Dahieh is the most densely populated area in Lebanon, home to more than a million people. Approximately 90% of them are Shia. While Amal, the other Shia party, also has broad support, Dahieh is known as a Hezbollah stronghold. In the last decade, I have been lucky enough to work in some fascinating places, including cities in Kurdistan where the PKK is hegemonic, rural areas of Colombia controlled by guerrillas or paramilitaries, Palestinian refugee camps, Serb enclaves in Kosovo, and Ukraine in the first month of the war. But nowhere else have I ever witnessed such impressive and effective territorial control as that exercised by Hezbollah in Dahieh and the country's south. The first time I became aware of this was on my first visit to the location at the heart of this article: the Rawdat Al Shahidain cemetery, a vast mausoleum dedicated to Hezbollah's martyrs.

The first thing that strikes you there is that the tombs look more like posters. They feature a mixture of religious elements, photographs of the dead dressed in military uniforms and bearing arms, lights in a variety of colours, and flowers, both natural and artificial. The highest ranks in the hierarchy have the biggest and most eye-catching graves. Imad Mugniyah, the intelligence chief known as "the Leader of the Two Victories", in reference to the liberation of southern Lebanon in 2000 and the 2006 war, has the privilege of being buried in the largest pantheon alongside one of his sons and his mother. Hadi Nasrallah, son of Secretary-General Hassan Nasrallah, is buried there, and there are also some Hezbollah allies who were not members, such as Mohammed Abdel Malik al-Shami, the spiritual leader of the Houthis in Yemen.

When Hezbollah decided to enter the Syrian war in 2013, the cemetery proved too small, so another even larger pavilion had to be built a few metres away. The second enclosure is less spectacular than the first. Most of the tombstones are smaller, and there is less variety.

But probably because the dead are more recent, it is more crowded. Groups of women, especially the wives and sisters of martyrs, gather there to pray, console each other and keep their memory alive, both in the familial and political sense.

The concept of martyrs is not unique to Hezbollah nor to Shia Islam. In the Muslim world as a whole, martyr is a polysemous word that refers both to the fallen soldier in jihad and, by extension, to any unjust victim of conflict. The term takes on particular relevance in the Middle East and, these days, more specifically in Palestine, where it is used to describe the men, women and children, combatants or civilians, killed at the hands of the Israeli occupation army. But to understand the genealogy of its current use in Palestine, we must go back to the neighbouring country of Lebanon, specifically to 1989.

Hamas was created in 1987. Two years later, it killed the first two Israeli soldiers. This resulted in a life sentence for Sheikh Ahmed Yasin, the movement's founder, and the deportation of 400 cadres to Lebanon. There, Hamas militants began to weave their alliance with Hezbollah. Their religious differences were striking: Hamas is Sunni and has its roots in the international Muslim Brotherhood, while Hezbollah, founded five years earlier, is Shia. But the existence of a powerful common enemy, Israel, prompted them to forge closer ties. What began with military strategy meetings soon evolved into a much closer relationship in which Hamas became imbued with the martyrdom cult of its new allies.

The concept of martyrdom in Hezbollah's ideology is fundamentally political. But it is indivisible from Shia theology, which dates back to the 7th-century battle of Karbala and the auspicious martyrdom of the Prophet Muhammad's grandson, Imam Hussain, considered an icon of resistance and sacrifice. In the traditional interpretation of martyrdom, the martyr is rewarded with a special status in Islam. The founder of the Islamic Revolution, Imam Khomeini, said, "Our nation looks forward to an opportunity for self-sacrifice and martyrdom; as such, red death is much better than black life." Moreover, Hezbollah's Secretary-General Sayyed Hassan Nasrallah stated, "Our people in Palestine, as in Lebanon, possess a substantial power; they are lovers of martyrdom, lovers of meeting God."

The importance of martyrdom also implies a duty to pay tribute to their memory. Even though Hezbollah's ideology could, evidently, be defined as conservative from a certain point of view, it is common for Shia leaders to exhort their followers to be innovative in their jihad. "Jihad" here is understood as a religious concept that goes far beyond the caricature often associated in the West with the word because of terrorist Sunni organisations such as Al-Qaida or ISIS, who in Hezbollah parlance are referred to as Takfiris (a false Muslim that accuses a true Muslim of apostasy). One area where this desire for innovation is central is in the commemoration of the martyrs.

Authoring books, producing films and providing memorial services for martyrs are actions encouraged by the elites of Iran and, to a lesser extent, Hezbollah. But where the Lebanese party is truly pioneering is in the construction of the tombs of its fallen, as we have seen. Yet the monumental aspect of martyrdom extends far beyond the tombstones. Portraits of the martyrs populate every corner of the villages in the south and the Beqaa Valley, the two areas most loyal to Hezbollah besides Dahieh. It is impossible to take a walk, go shopping, go to school, or simply drive around without seeing the faces of the fallen. If you pay attention, you will also learn about their military exploits, profusely explained by posters in places where, for example, the Israeli army was ambushed.

One could argue that every army and every political movement in the world worships its fallen. That may be true. But very few places go so far as to create a theme park. The Museum for Resistance Tourism, its official name, was opened in 2010 in Mleeta in southern Lebanon, on one of the hills where Hezbollah dug tunnels and operated using guerrilla techniques during the Israeli occupation of the south.

Due to its worship of martyrs, Hezbollah is labelled by its enemies as a death-loving cult because its adherents place no value on life. They describe them as fanatics who don't care whether they live or die. Supporters of the Party of God vehemently deny this and point out that the vast majority of martyrs are from the Shia elite, i.e., the middle class, not those who don't enjoy a decent quality of life. Most of the fighters are highly educated, own businesses or land, and have aspirations and ambitions. In other words, for them, resting in peace in tombs adorned with multi-coloured LEDs is not an imposition from above; it is a privilege.

Where detractors and supporters alike agree is on the importance of the mothers. They are the ones who instil the values of abnegation and dignity in them. They believe that when a patriotic hero sacrifices his life, he secures that of the whole community. I once questioned two relatives of Hezbollah martyrs on the subject: Ibtisan, a neighbour in southern Lebanon who fell victim to an Israeli drone as she and her family tried to escape from the south in a civilian bus (many died; she came close), and Rabiha, the sister of a fighter. Both denied that their families, and they themselves, do not value life. "We love life, but only a dignified life is worth living," Ibtisan told me. "Those who accuse us of being death-worshippers are very wrong," said Rabiha, "we love life. That is precisely why my brother went to fight and became a martyr."

السلام عليك يا سيدي ويا مولاي يا أبا عبد الله الحسين
وعلى الأرواح التي حلت بفنائك وأناخت برحلك عليك مني سلام
ولادة 17/2/1994
استشهاد 4/6/2013

كلنا عباسك يا زينب
الشهيد المجاهد
محمد علي اسعد الحاج حسين
شهداؤنا
أسمى غاية الجود
الشهيد المجاهد
حسين علي اسماعيل

يا أبا الفضل العباس (ع)
الشهيد المجاهد
السيد علي أحمد اسماعيل
(ذو الفقار)
حسين

الشهيد
القائد الجهادي الكبير
السيد مصطفى بدر الدين
الحسين
الطفل الرضيع
علي الأكبر
شهيد الدفاع المقدس
محمد حسن عزقول
(غريب)
الشهيد القائد
الحاج عباس حسين حمود
(الحاج أحمد المخ)
تفاحتا
محمد
لينا
يارا

END THE OC

SOLIDARITY

لا سلام

Designed and printed by Ariadna Serrahima and Lara Coromina in collaboration with Dania Shihab, Simon Williams, Ailo Ribas, Diego Bustamante and Ferran Fandos. Thanks to all our friends and comrades who have helped to circulate and distribute it since mid-October 2023. Printed at L'Automàtica, Barcelona.

STOP THE

CUPATION

لا عدالة

GENOCIDE

WITH PALESTINE

An interview with Ben Yart by Hans Laguna

DRINK WATER, BRO

Images by Alexandra Cepeda

Ben Yart and I are sitting face to face in a bar near Barcelona's Mar Bella beach. We order two beers. I turn on the recorder. We soon realise that the place is too noisy for the chat to be recorded properly. Ben Yart gets up and goes over to the waiter to ask him to turn down the television. He does so in the perfect tone, firm but polite. He then asks a man sitting at the bar to turn down the ring tone on his mobile, which has just been ringing at a thunderous volume. The man obliges, and Ben Yart responds with a "gracias, rey". The situation could easily have sparked tension, but he handled it beautifully. He clearly has a way with people. "I always land on my feet", he'll tell me later.
To warm up, I explain that VISIONS BY is a magazine published in English and distributed internationally. I ask him what impression he thinks readers who don't know him and don't understand Spanish will get of him.

BY That's where you come in.
HL Sure, but what do you think they'll think when they hear your music but don't understand your lyrics?
BY It'll wholly depend on your input.
HL Okay then, I'm going to go for the easy option and put what's on your record company's website: "Ben Yart is a kid from Mendillorri, in Pamplona, who translates his day-to-day life into his music. And he doesn't hide. He deals unashamedly with subjects like drugs, life in the neighbourhood and the wildness of the fiestas".
BY Amen to that! Go ahead.

Yes, Ben Yart talks about drugs. Lots of them. Almost all of them. But if I have to explain who Ben Yart is to readers who don't know him, I would say that he also talks about the class struggle while walking his dog **→ SEARCH FOR: [Spotify] Ceros - Gallery session.** And of the gratitude he feels for the squatters' movement, which took him in when he moved to Barcelona **→ SEARCH FOR: [Spotify] Gracias a Pi.** He's also the type of guy who always gives the impression that he's doing whatever he wants. And that musically, he uses trap, but also lo-fi intimacy with guitar **→ SEARCH FOR: [Youtube] Me tomau tus alprazolames q beneno porfabor no recomiendo** or the psychedelic-quinqui melange **→ SEARCH FOR: [Spotify] Me keke kedau.** What I would say, though, is that he takes it all in his stride. There's a reason Ben Yart is considered a master of shitposting and a point of reference for how to become a meme with brilliance and dignity. And I'm going to start by asking him precisely about the character he's created for himself.

HL How do you understand the relationship between person and character? In the lyrics of "Desnudo" **→ SEARCH FOR: [Youtube] Ben Yart Desnudo**, you sing, "I won't be eaten by the role of Ben Yart / in fact, it will eat my dick." Is that still the case?
BY Yes. It's about the character working for you rather than you working for it. You have to understand your role as if you were a clown. You don't want to be that clown when you're at home in your living room.
HL Don't you think that the role you play influences you?
BY No, to be honest, not much. I put on the character when I want to, if I need to. When I'm short of the money to catch a bus, I walk around, and if I see someone who recognises me, I go up to them and say, "Yo, bro, I've been left stranded". And it's the same with everything, with drugs, everything. Then, in reality, when I don't feel like playing the role, even if other people miss it, I'm not going to play it.
HL For example, in the photo session, who were you?
BY I was Beñat [his real name]. I was Beñat trying to get some good photos for Ben Yart.
HL And now, in this interview?
BY Now I'm Beñat trying to do a good interview for Ben Yart. For example, what I just asked these guys [referring to turning down the volume on the TV and phone a few minutes ago], Beñat did that, man. Ben Yart isn't supposed to care.
HL Talk about schizophrenia!
BY Not at all! It's a game. It's like going to the circus and being a clown. But when I say clown, it's not with that connotation of being ridiculous that the word clown sometimes gets given; it's just that a clown understands how to separate things well. And if he doesn't, his wife commits suicide. Imagine having a clown in your living room... On the other hand, a magician, for example, doesn't know how to separate things, and he might be in the living room and suddenly try to do a magic trick on you, you know? Imagine what a fucking embarrassment for his wife.
HL So why not just compare it to being an actor?
BY Because an actor has lots of different roles. But, well, the guy from the TV show Friends supposedly lost his mind and thought he was his character. So many years of playing the same character…
HL Like Bela Lugosi, the actor who played Count Dracula in the thirties and that was it, he was typecast, making loads of films in the same style. And he ended up in a bad way. They buried him dressed as Dracula, with the cloak and everything.
BY I think it might be more because his persona didn't have its own appeal. And so, when he wasn't Dracula, he missed being Dracula. And he needed to remind everybody that he was Dracula.
HL I've got loads of questions. And they're not in much of an order.
BY Go ahead. I do better than anyone in chaos.
HL So, let's talk about social networks. You're very active on them. Do you make a conscious effort to work on them? Is it more of a spontaneous thing, or is there an idea behind it?
BY I feel like I understand them really well. I understand how it all works. The concepts. The brands. And if I was a bit more disciplined, I could make people believe that I'm God on earth on the Internet.
HL But how much do you think about the image you project on the networks?
BY If I've been affected by something, I'll say, "damn, these days I need to be more organised", and I'll upload a picture of my room with my freshly made bed. That's the trick. For example, you're Tiger Woods, and you've just been caught up in an infidelity scandal. That's when you have to run your social networks like an orderly, loyal, faithful person. Upload a picture of your kids, all that fucking shit.
HL So, would you like someone to manage your social media for you?
BY Yes, I'd like someone to help me,

but I don't want someone to do it for me. I might have a hard time dealing with a picture that someone else has uploaded of me if I don't like the way my face looks or if I'm angry because my beard has bald patches; who knows? So, I'd call them and until they deleted the photo, I wouldn't stop calling them, and if they didn't delete it, I'd get everyone to denounce it en masse.

HL And how do you control the photos and videos people take of you at concerts?

BY At concerts, it doesn't bother me because unless the photo is good, it won't transcend. The issue is when it's uploaded to a medium where a lot of people will see it, and you look ugly in that photo.

HL In other words, you exercise control over your image.

BY I don't exercise it until I suddenly see something that pisses me off, and then I don't stop until it's deleted.

HL "I don't know what I want but I know what I don't want."

BY Exactly [laughter], I get that a lot when I record a song in a studio, too. I need to listen to it before I leave the studio and make sure it's to my liking because otherwise, from a distance, I'm going to drive the producer crazy. I might ask for 200 different changes with things that I'm not happy with, and, of course, that's a nightmare for a producer. That's why I've learned to use all the sequencers: FL Studio, Ableton Logic, Cubase... Also, you can annoy him if you're there in front of him all the time asking him to change such and such a thing in such and such a minute... So, it's better to say to him, "let me have a moment now". Another thing is that in the studio, I go into these trances where everything goes fast. I'm very clear about how each rendition has to sound, and I can drive you crazy doing a lot of takes. Can you bring us another two, *rey*? [he asks the waiter for two more beers].

HL I'm going to jump to another topic, delve into messier topics. I'm going to push you.

BY No problem; push me. Let's see what you've got. [He picks up my script and reads some questions about selling out to capitalism.] Talking about selling out? You think that's pushing me? You must have something worse than that for me...

HL Actually, I do. We're going to talk about your relationship with masculinity.

BY Uff, that's a good one [laughter].

HL While we're at it, I want to ask you about your relationship with brands. I can't recall seeing you associated with any brand...

BY So that's because I've done a bad job, to be honest. I'm trying to get myself associated with [clothing brand we'll call X].

HL Does X give you free clothes?

BY They gave me a tracksuit. Then I tried to manipulate them. I told them that I had been wearing that tracksuit for two weeks, that my girlfriend was worried and that they had to give me something else. So, they sent me another one. And then a friend of mine bought me a third tracksuit from X and I made out that the brand had given it to me to get them thinking. This is why I use social networks: to get tracksuits.

HL Would you do adverts or agree to more direct exposure?

BY Yeah, I would have to read the script, but I don't have a problem with that. It would also depend on what the advert is for. I wouldn't advertise holiday resorts in Israel.

HL And an advert for Z [name of a major Spanish bank]?

BY Depending on how much money they give me, I'd hold my nose, cover my eyes and get on with it.

HL Do you think that your lyrics and your defence of drugs have worked against you when it comes to getting sponsors?

BY Yes, of course. I've never really defended drugs. But just living in a universe where drugs exist or having made any allusion to them or their effects, already puts you in a different category. You mentioned the Z bank. Well, obviously, everyone who works for Z has had their experience with drugs, and drugs do exist in their universe. But, of course, in that world, you have to pretend they don't exist. In other words, talking about drugs is like saying on live TV that the Three Kings [the equivalent to Santa Claus for Spanish children] don't exist. It takes you right out of prime time.

HL How do you interpret the fact that there is a kind of pact of silence in mainstream music on the subject of drugs?

BY I don't know. To be honest, these are complicated issues. I understand all the posturing about drugs not existing on TV. I also have those limits in my head. The truth is that when I started making music, I didn't think that so many people would listen to it, you know? I don't want to talk about cocaine when my nephew can hear me, right?

HL So, now we come to the issue of selling yourself. Does the idea suggest anything to you? Do you think there is an authenticity that can be sold to brands or to capitalism? Have you experienced any conflicts like that?

BY None. A bigger conflict than when, for example, I was a waiter in a bar, and I was pretty much exploited and accepted conditions that were shit for me, no; no conflicts bigger than that.

HL Have you not experienced any moral conflicts in your profession?

BY The whole Israel thing is weighing pretty heavily on my mind these days. That is something I think about. Nowadays, I think that if a brand called me, I would do a bit of homework on its relationship with the issue. Although I know that if the brand is from the Anglo-Saxon culture or its colonies, it'll be involved in some form or another...

HL I'm glad to hear that. But let's change the subject completely and talk about your amazing hair. Long male hair is normally associated with heavy metal or grunge but not with urban music. To what extent is it a distinguishing feature for you? What significance do you attach to it?

BY I think the conception we have in our heads is that a man with long hair is making it clear that he hasn't done his military service. It comes from that, from the fact that in the '60s anyone with long hair was showing that he hadn't done military service. It is an act of insubordination. It gives off this vibe that says, "this son of a bitch is outside the system and does whatever he wants". **→ SEARCH FOR: [Enciclopedia.com] Long hair for men**

HL Is it a symbol of rebellion?

BY Not of rebellion, of years in the act of rebelling! Not everything that is outside the system is rebellion. There's also banishment... What's the word for it? Being an outcast for a long time, left out of society...

HL Ostracism?

BY That's it. To be ostracised. Long hair indicates ostracism or rebelliousness for more than three or four years, which is how long it takes to grow. That's the image that long hair conveys. And when I've got a gig, I brush it out and it's crazy.

HL And isn't there also an interplay between the macho act of taking your shirt off and showing your biceps and the long hair associated with femininity? You're playing a bit of a game with that, right?

BY It's like you act like you can be everything.

HL You've got the best of both worlds.

BY Yes. It's like here in Barcelona I hang out with a lot of queers and trannies, and I think that's where I got it from. From La Sailor **→ SEARCH FOR: [Instagram] @sailor.ya**. I wish La Sailor was a well-known character. Then you'd know what I mean straight away. Let's see if I can find her on Instagram... She's a transvestite who's also a total babe. In fact, in her bio, it says, "A hot mess with the best of both worlds". A queer with long hair. And I think that's where that self-demand came from. [He shows me her Instagram] She's my friend. She's a crazy bitch. When she models, she's brilliant! When she raps, she's brilliant! She's a fucking diva.

HL It looks like she was made by AI.

BY It's unbelievable. She's a total badass. Yeah, so this thing about having the best of both worlds is influenced by them. That's how I've discovered the swag in having great hair and a more rogue intelligence.

HL But from a straight perspective, right?

BY Yeah... Well, no, at the moment I'm not being straight or anything. I'm glowing.

HL Isn't there some form of appropriation there?

BY No, because I'm not saying that I'm a queer, and I'm not playing with being bisexual or anything like that. I'm talking about a person who's a model in some photos and a Justin Bieber in others, and I'm playing with that a bit... Being Justin Bieber doesn't look as good on me, and being a babe, even less so, but that's where the idea of having great hair comes from. And, anyway, there's also the fact that the top artists have always been a bit ambiguous in terms of genre. All that glam metal and those guys who wore tights...

HL And David Bowie.

BY For me, David Bowie was a phenomenal, phenomenal man. Although David Bowie might have been queerer, I think the person who's played on the whole thing the most is that guy from Guns n' Roses; what's his name?

HL Axl Rose.

BY Axl Rose has achieved more of that femininity [he picks up his mobile and shows me photos of Axl Rose as a young man] than David Bowie, even though he wears God knows what kind of shoes. We order two more beers and turn to the next topic: physical exercise.

HL When I first discovered you, I was surprised to see you in stories doing pull-ups or showing off your muscles. I thought to myself: is this guy really a fitness fan, or is it part of the character? What's going on there?

BY Sport is vital, man. Being a person who moves is vital. I know what I'm saying is a cliché. But yeah, man. Your machine has to be active. I mean, you get into sport for other reasons, but then I swear you stick with it because it feels good, man. For me, it's mainly because of my ADHD; I need mini achievements all the time. And a killer mini achievement is to say, "right, now do 15 push-ups". And you can count them. Sport can be counted, while all the other great things in life can't be. And for me, it's really good to set out to do 15 push-ups and do 15 push-ups.

HL I know quite a few musicians who do 6 grams of coke at the weekend and then work out in the gym on Monday to clear their conscience.

BY In my case, it's not that it clears my conscience; it's that it's good for me, man. Since I know a little bit about nutrition, if I'm partying and taking drugs like hell for three days, I'll drink water for those three days. And I'll nag my mates to drink water. On my Instagram, I used to call myself "Bebe agua, bro" ["Drink water, bro"]. It's really fucking good for me to have like a bodybuilding mentality. I'm not saying bigorexia. I'm saying bodybuilding, which is knowing about nutrition and the nervous system.

HL And what have you learned?

BY That drug-related erection problems come from dehydration. Some things are vasodilators, which open up your veins so that everything flows better, and some things are vasoconstrictors, which tighten them. And drugs tighten them.

HL There used to be a morning TV programme [in Spain] called *Saber vivir* [Knowing how to live] that gave health advice to grandparents. **→ SEARCH FOR: [Youtube] Saber vivir con Manuel Torreiglesias**

BY Yeah, brother, bring back *Saber vivir*, bring back *Saber vivir*! But knowing how to live shouldn't just be for older people. Everyone should know how to live. It's good to know how to live.

HL [Laughter] Who can deny that it is good to know how to live? Talk about demagogy!

BY Of course, it's demagogy. But there's demagogy, and there's the truth. And what I am saying is the truth. This is a whole new level of demagogy, right? I can promise and I do promise that knowing how to live is good! [Laughter]

HL Let's continue with the theme of body awareness, but in terms of excesses. There's a line in "Me Keke Kedau" that I love: "El cuerpo te da señales/ diarrea en los matorrales" [The body gives you signs / diarrhoea in the bushes"].

BY [Laughter] It's brilliant.

HL And it goes on: "When something is bad for you and you keep taking it / throwing stones at your own roof."

BY See what I mean, man? Does that sound like a defence of drugs to you? I'm talking about my mates there. There's also this thing about drugs, which is that when you have a drug problem, you look for someone who has a worse drug problem than you and you give them advice. That's not knowing how to live. That's an endemic evil that I suffer from.

HL Have you become more addicted to drugs as a musician? Is there something about being a musician that makes you indulge in more excesses?

BY Maybe, yes, because to be honest, whenever I need something, I can get it. And people are always happy to invite me. I've always known how to say no to drugs because I started with drugs by selling them. But there are people that get into the music scene with a say yes to everything attitude and... it's a problem! I, for example, don't do coke. It doesn't agree with me, cocaine makes me feel bad; it gives me anxiety.

HL And speed doesn't?

BY No, speed doesn't make me anxious. Speed puts me in my place. It focuses me.

HL I get that with joints.

BY I smoke joints too, but they give me anxiety, man.

HL Even when they're made with hashish?

BY All of them. Even CBD, I swear. Even tobacco gives me anxiety. It's probably mostly somatised.

HL And coffee?

BY No, coffee makes me feel great, it makes me feel incredible.

HL You said before that you have ADHD.

BY Yes. Coffee's really good for my ADHD. The thing about ADHD is that you constantly need rewards for everything you do. You need dopamine all the time.

HL And sex?

BY Sex is affected by ADHD as well. If I'm very ADHD, my mind can't focus on the sex.

HL That must be shit.

BY Yeah, it's shit, but I've got my resources too. For example, I focus more on her for a while, and when I've won those prizes, like seeing her enjoying herself, then I get into the groove.

HL I'm going to link this to another topic...

BY Watch out... here comes the link of the year!

HL What's the deal with love songs? I don't know all your work, but after a quick skim, I have yet to find any. The closest thing to romanticism is a phrase in "Satisfayer" that says, "sometimes your eyes / my dick doesn't deserve them". Within the decrepitude of the lyrics of that song, I thought it was beautiful.

BY Yeah, I play with that a bit.

HL What is your conception of romantic love songs?

BY I love them. But they have to be good, man. I'm not running away, I swear. Among the songs I haven't released, there are a lot of love songs. Really good ones, too. It's just a coincidence that they haven't been released... And also, because I'm more of a perfectionist with love songs. I am the best lover. My girlfriends know that. The things I say to them! I'm a poet. That being loved by me is like being fucked by Nacho Vidal. → **SEARCH FOR: [xvideos.com] Nacho Vidal**

HL I think you're someone who raises very key issues, who has a knack for touching the bone, but always with an ironic package, meta, meme... To me this suggests a generational fear of expressing emotions directly.

BY That's true.

HL There are flashes of deep emotion, but they're neutralised by the clown.

BY It's a bit like "hey, don't worry, I'm not really being profound, relax, stay".

HL Maybe not for three hours, but for three minutes?

BY Three minutes in a song is three hours in a living room.

HL Actually, I do remember one of your songs → **SEARCH FOR: [Genius] Dejen de romantizar la duda** where you talk about your mother's worldview and compare it to yours. And you say things like, "mama wanted to know the truth / I just want to get drunk / mama thought she knew the truth / I only know how to doubt / and that makes me so weak, so fragile". And you end with "Their generation killed God, who am I going to kill?". I was surprised by the subject and the way it was handled.

BY When I made that song, I was arguing with my dad and my brother, and I told them that we're going to be worse off than the previous generation. And they said, "bollocks to that". Well, hell yeah, kid!

HL So, I didn't find any irony in that song. It can only be understood in one way.

BY When I've opened up a lot, I get very attached to those songs, and it's hard for me to release them because they have to be finished to fucking perfection.

HL In other words, you only release what you couldn't give a shit about.

BY [Laughter] Yeah. [He becomes pensive] Nowadays, all this cringe stuff is making people lose a bit of purity. 'This is cringe, this isn't cringe'... Ultimately, there's no one expressing themselves purely, even if it's embarrassing.

HL And to round things off: isn't the ironic attitude working for the system? Isn't it a way of depoliticising us? For fear of the cringe, you stop getting involved.

BY Well, in the case of politics, I think it's more because you're afraid that nobody will follow you, right? If you call a demonstration or go around saying that "this has to stop now" ... There's also a touch of thinking you're a hero, isn't there?

HL Maybe other people think you're right.

BY Depends. It's just that not everyone is always at the same point at the same time. I think revolutions happen because, at a given moment, coincidentally, everybody's hormones start firing at the same time, making them all very pissed off. Revolutions happen when everyone is pissed off at the same time.

HL But look at what's happening with Palestine .**→ SEARCH FOR: [Google] Israel's genocide of the Palestinian people**

BY And what are we doing? Are we all going to Israel?

HL In my environment, I'm seeing people posting about Palestine who have never shared anything about geopolitics...

BY There might be a spike there, yes.

HL I told you I was finishing, but it wasn't true.

BY Don't worry, man, I'm comfortable, honestly.

He heads to the bathroom, and I take the opportunity to order another round of beers. He comes back.

BY I drank some water, just like that! Water with calcium carbonate. It's disgusting.

HL Barcelona tap water is terrible.

BY Is it drinkable or not?

HL Yes.

BY There you go then. What's terrible is not drinking water.

HL The title of the interview should be "Drink water, bro".

BY "Bebe agua, bro". It was my best name.

HL Right, more questions. The issue of ambition and the obligation to grow as an artist. It seems that one is obliged to grow because if you stay at one level, others will step on your toes, and you'll disappear.

BY Yes, also because the campaign of a person who's been stagnating for a long time starts to become tiresome.

HL It seems like if you stop for a minute, everything will go to shit. Is that how you see it?

BY I don't think my campaign relies on me pushing myself all the time. For example, the 'Gucci Gang, Gucci Gang, Gucci Gang' campaign, that guy [referring to Lil Pump]... **→ SEARCH FOR: [Youtube] Gucci Gang** His campaign did rely on him pushing himself. OK, now you're selling us that yesterday you lived in a caravan and now you live in a Lambo. But what are you going to sell us tomorrow? I remember that in *Tú sí que vales* [a Spanish reality TV show like Got talent], in the first phase, they said to them: "What you're doing is very nice, but what are you going to do in the second phase?"

HL And you don't feel like disappearing for a while? Spend three weeks without posting anything? Is there a fear of being pushed into a corner by the algorithm?

BY If I disappeared right now, the only thing I would achieve would be to increase my hype.

HL So, what's stopping you?

BY Because I'm happy. Instagram and Twitter entertain me. I don't feel like "I have to upload something, I have to upload something". I'm pretty free of that pressure. I know it exists and stuff, but personally, I'm pretty free of it.

HL Now this is definitely the last block. We're going to finish on a downer. Let's talk about growing old. In "Desnudo" you say, "I'll live without fear of being fat or bald".

BY Fat and bald? [Laughter] Fuck, what a beast. I didn't know I said fat and bald.

HL How do you imagine yourself getting older? In your style of music, there are no role models. In rock, there is, I don't know, the Rolling Stones, but in the urban scene, there's nobody old.

BY You're right, that's true. You know what's left for me? To be that role model. To be that Rolling Stone. And if there comes a time when people feel sorry for me, but I'm still on the circuit, it'll be because I'm making money.

HL Pity that makes money.

BY Or that, despite being pitiful, I make money.

HL So, are you worried about getting older?

BY It does worry me. Look, Johnny Paycheck has a country song called "The Old Violin" **→ SEARCH FOR: [Spotify] Paycheck old violin,** in which he says he feels like an old violin that nobody wants to play anymore. And just doing that song about being an old violin that nobody wants to play anymore was cooler than ever. He made a song with his point of view from that moment; he didn't try to be the cowboy he was when he was 25. He said, "shit, I'm not cool anymore" and made a song that made him rock.

HL And that gives you hope.

BY Yeah, right now, from here, yeah. When I'm a Johnny Paycheck, who knows... Anyway, I think the thing that'll worry me when I'm older is my back. I don't think I'll worry too much about whether I'm cool or not. My back, my knees... My sexual impotence.

HL But if you drink water, your impotence will be cured.

BY No, when you're that old, it's all about hormones...

HL And the hair? Are you worried about losing it?

BY It's not an issue. My grandfather went bald at 90. And my father is 70 and he's got more hair than...

HL Look at that, we're done! Let's hope that everything has recorded...

BY If it hasn't recorded, we'll do it again tomorrow, right?

HL The same interview again?

BY No, you ask me the same questions and who knows where I'll go with them.

Gabriel Calvin

SHOP-LIFTING: A HIDDEN HISTORY OF THE POCKET

The law locks up the man or woman
Who steals the goose off the common
But leaves the greater villain loose
Who steals the common from the goose.
17th century folk poem

It is more dignified to beg than to work,
but it is more edifying to steal than to beg.
Jean Genet

Shoplifting is a phenomenon that became exponentially popular with the rise of modernity, the crystallization of the Industrial Revolution and the emergence of department stores in Europe. The term, in fact, is of English origin, and begins to appear in some documents as early as the 16th century, referring to shoplifters.[1] During the proliferation of department stores in the Victorian era in England, it became current again and was commonly included in the legal glossary, for the first time, to refer to female thieves who frequented the stores, mostly from the wealthy classes.

Theft in this case signified a gesture of autonomy and an assumption of power in the face of the economic control exercised by men as householders. Thus, women appropriated the merchandise they considered attractive and necessary to maintain their status without asking permission from their husbands at the same time as they appropriated the space that allowed them to interact outside the patriarchal domestic cell.

From this widespread illegal phenomenon, kleptomania[2] emerged for the first time, originally defined as a mental illness associated with femininity, which served mainly as a legal device to protect these "respectable" women belonging to the middle and upper classes from prison sentences, while harshly criminalizing those of working class origin.[3] In one case, the justice system understood that the theft was the result of caprice and the penalty was minimized, and in the other, the result of necessity, it was punished with imprisonment and forced labor.[4]

It was the women of this Victorian era who were the first to transform and personalize clothing as a technology capable, on the one hand, of serving as camouflage —to pass themselves off as solvent shoppers— and, at the same time, of hiding merchandise inside.[5]

At the same time and on an international level, what has come to be known as expropriative anarchism[6] emerged from the anarcho-individualist current. From the anarchist movement, motivated by the burnout of trade union activity, small affinity groups began to organize themselves and take direct action a step further by obtaining financing and resources that did not come from the fruits of labor exploitation, but from bank robberies, robberies in luxury stores, thefts in department stores or the forgery of bank checks. With these gestures, anarchists protested against the unequal distribution of wealth and underlined that the creation of private property and wage labor were the ultimate expressions of theft.[7]

Expropriative anarchism in this sense also made a sharp reappropriation of language, thus inverting the official meaning of the words "steal" and "expropriate," defending individual expropriation as a way of returning or restoring what was unduly taken away by the parasitism of the owner class.

This phenomenon is remarkable in order to contextualize that it will be the first time that a solid ethical discourse is constructed, legitimizing expropriation, which takes into account the specific characteristics in which it is circumscribed, questioning head-on the established legality and morality. Furthermore, following the theoretical line of Proudhon in *What Is Property?* it's possible to follow the trail of the historical processes of the enclosure of the commons,[8] which led to a generalized dispossession since the Industrial Revolution, and which continues to expand its logic of spoliation and colonization globally to the present.

Understanding from this perspective, that pillage and theft are structural characteristics of the capitalist system on an immense scale, it's also possible to trace a diversity of informal conscious practices of material and symbolic reappropriation in the opposite direction[9] towards a recovery of the economy of gift,[10] cooperation and commoning, among which shoplifting can be included as one of them.

As it is evident that access to the monetary flow is absolutely unfair, where the labor market on the one hand exploits and creates scarcity with poverty wages while on the other hand directly excluding large segments of the population from it, it is possible to conceive of shoplifting as a tool that is available to partially solve the economic limitations imposed in accessing certain resources in urbanized areas.

Without losing sight of the fact that shoplifting is an action that has defined limits as it does not offer an alternative to the dominant economic system, and being aware that it is not a skill that is available to everyone —since there are also structural inequalities that intervene when it comes to performing it— it could still be claimed as a shared tactic that serves to gain some ground against the extreme commodification of our lives.

Despite the fact that shoplifting is a gesture that, although exercised without political intentionality, is in itself political, it can also be read as an alternative form of individualized consumption.

Regardless, it has the capacity to function as a form of active boycott, allowing the possibility of saving money for other more pressing needs or supporting other types of productive structures based on principles of self-management.[11] Far from romanticizing shoplifting as a true form of revolutionary action, it is preferable to rethink more extensively about its potential and limitations.[12] In general, when expropriation acquires a collective projection, its disruptive and transformative power is amplified.[13] Delving deeper into the features of the activity, one can observe its potential as an empowering practice. Apart from its main motivation, which solves material scarcity, the practice provides a variety of knowledge and skills that broaden personal agency, expanding the limits of what is possible through transgression.

In the improvement of the technique, creativity and inventiveness are applied to solve problems, understand limitations, find weak points and blind spots, make tools, reformulate pre-existing objects,[14] study surveillance routines or explore the city through an alternative cartography that does not respond to the pre-established functions of architecture or urbanism, thus overflowing the utilitarian use of the city constrained to production and consumption.[15]

Contemporary metropolises are being progressively emptied of their community life to be transformed into large centers of consumption, thus neutralizing their capacity for emancipation or free social interaction.[16] Through practices such as shoplifting, these non-places[17] of a submissive, excluding and boring nature can be re-signified and reappropriated in a temporary and symbolic way, as a sort of playground[18] where one can have fun without paying admission, thus creating new itineraries of use for which these spaces were never designed.

Echoing the proposals and attempts of autonomy of the avant-gardes to merge art with everyday life and to reclaim artisticity outside the limits of the art industry and its professional specialization, it can be extracted that pilfering could be considered an artistic practice for making use of imagination and creativity to solve the real problems of everyday life in a playful way. Along this line, it is worth mentioning groups such as The Diggers in San Francisco, who used shoplifting as a political and performative tool, inspired by guerrilla theater, to collectivize the practice and reclaim the gratuitousness. In parallel and on the East Coast, very similar actions were carried out by the Yippies.[19] Already in the new millennium, the YoMango collective recovered the energy of these groups to actualize shoplifting more concretely as a form halfway between art and festive revolt to extend their practice and serve at the same time as a laboratory for learning new ways of collective living within their context.

Assuming that the implementation of money as a method of exchange is rather an imposition that protects the social order,[20] then, to resist its constant mediation means at the same time to get rid of its artifice. Taking things without paying responds to a very intuitive form of demanding the gratuity of things, for a symbolic return to the commons. It is a gesture of civil disobedience and rejection that interrupts the social contract and the economy of exchange, making it possible, in the last instance, to satisfy needs that should be guaranteed beforehand for human beings simply due to the fact of existing.

1 In 1591, playwright Robert Greene published a pamphlet titled "The Second Part of Cony Catching," in which he described how three men could conspire to shoplift clothes and fabric from London merchants.

2 The Swiss doctor André Matthey coined the term klopémaniè in 1816 as a means to describe the impulsive urge to steal. Since then, criminologists genderized the crime as a feminine psychosexual disorder. In 1962, kleptomania was included in the DSM as a mental disorder and continues to serve as a way to pathologize and erase the social origins behind it.

3 The Forty Thieves gang is an example of working-class female thieves who, posing as wealthy women, infiltrated department stores to steal. The gang used social conventions, disguising themselves as wealthy women, to go unnoticed and get the job done.

4 The anarcha-feminist Emma Goldman denounced this classism during a speech she gave in Pittsburgh in 1896: "If a rich woman is caught shoplifting, the rich court has a new word for her and says she is afflicted with 'klepto-mania' and pities her."

5 Illustrated examples of different theft technologies can be found in the research: "The Mechanics of Shoplifting" by Silvia Bombardini.

6 "The Anarchist Expropriators: Buenaventura Durruti and Argentina's Working-Class Robin Hoods" by Osvaldo Bayer.

7 Anarchists understood that wage labor was a coercive form of slavery which at the same time served towards the accumulation of capital by the bourgeoisie. A central reference is "Theories of Surplus-Value" by Karl Marx.

8 "Caliban and the Witch: Women, The Body, and Primitive Accumulation" by Silvia Federici.

9 In the essay "The Practice of Everyday Life" De Certau focuses on the irreducibility of the human being to the great structures of power, his smallest, daily and imperceptible gestures of resistance.

10 A gift economy is a system of exchange where valuables are not sold, but rather given without an explicit agreement for immediate or future rewards. "The gift: Forms and functions of exchange in Archaic Societies" by Marcel Mauss.

11 Production co-ops are a form of association to organize work in a more horizontal and self-organized way. In any case, it is preferable to support small businesses that are in direct and unequal competition with the large distribution chains that abound in the cities.

12 "Shoplifting and the Politics of Instant Gratification. Are individual acts of transgression rebellion?" by Cookie Orlando. Fifth Estate #378, Summer 2008.

13 "Looting is a communal practice: it cannot be done alone. Anthropologist Neal Keating argues that looting creates a similar relation to property as the potlatch, a communal practice of Indigenous nations in the Pacific Northwest" [...] "Rioting and looting similarly redistribute and reduce the wealth and the surplus, leveling material power differentials" - "In Defense of Looting" by Vicky Osterweil.

14 Guy Debord, member of the Situationist movement, coined the term Détournement, which appeals to the artistic and political possibility of taking an object created by capitalism and distorting its original use to produce a critical effect. "Methods of Détournement" by Guy Debord.

15 It's captivating in this regard to review Geoff Manaugh's research "A Burglar's Guide to the City," on how burglars make an appropriation of architectural space for their own purposes.

16 The expansion of industrial society has provoked a sort of "urbicide," destroying the communal spaces of the rich social fabric and memory of the cities. In this direction the point of view in "The Death and Life of Great American Cities" by Jane Jacobs is very enlightening.

17 To get a deep understanding of the nature of these spaces, see "Non-places. Introduction to an anthropology of super modernity" by Marc Augé.

18 To think about this question of urban space as a place for leisure and free entertainment, an illustrative reference is "New Babylon" by Constant, an urban utopia where wage labor is abolished in favor of a life dedicated to fulfillment and freedom.

19 Abbie Hoffman published "Steal This Book," a reference manual that provided information on how to obtain any resource for free in New York City. Among his methods, he encouraged shoplifting.

20 A text that concisely and briefly illustrates how the production-consumption cycle works in capitalist societies is "The reproduction of Daily Life" by Fredy Perlman.

"I always feel like shoplifting"
Political graffiti on the top of a 7-Eleven in Copenhagen.

Anonymous inscription in Philadelphia supporting the lootings after the riots for the murder of George Floyd.

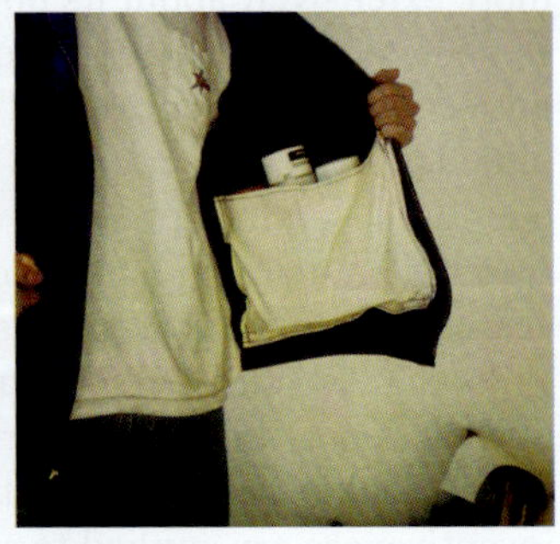
Custom-sewn pocket for "racking", the term is commonly used in the graffiti subculture to refer to shoplifting. San Francisco, CA, 1994. Craig Costello - Graffiti, Art, and Invention.

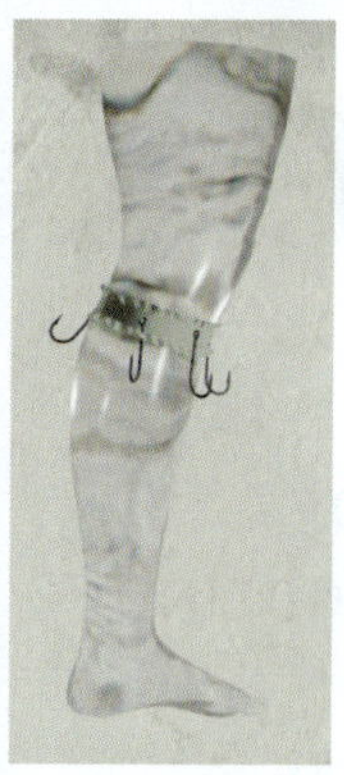

Reconstruction of shoplifting devices collected by Silvia Bombardini. 3D design by Sharif Elsabagh.

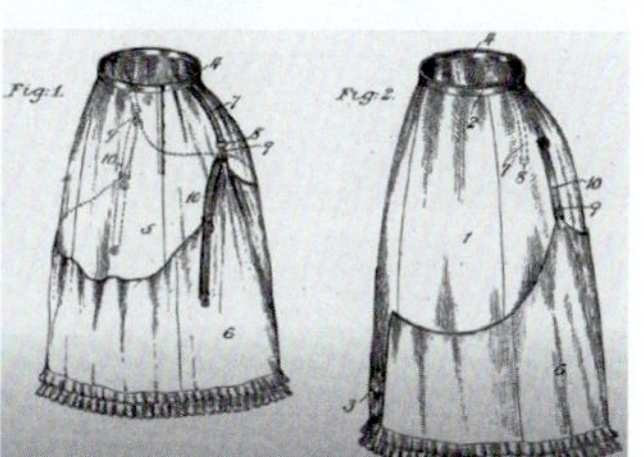

Petticoats were designed to have a large exterior pocket and could be used for shoplifting.

Caricature of the right-wing magazine Punch, where it reinforces the misogynist stereotype of the depraved woman thief, "sick" of kleptomania.

Faraday fabric is a metallic textile used to make bags and pockets to block radio frequencies emitted by RFID security tags. More rudimentary devices are made of foil paper.

Interiors of Harding Howell and Co. It was a 18th-century department store at 89 Pall Mall in St James's, London. Open from 1796 to 1820, it could be considered a forerunner of the modern department store.

Some drawings extracted from Steal This Book by Abbie Hoffman.

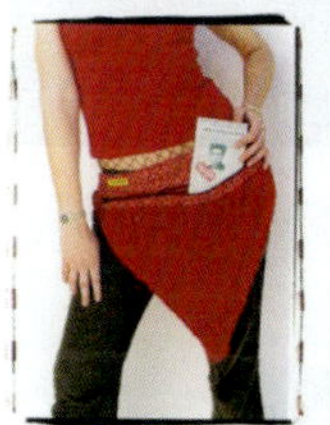

Outcomes of Yomango pocket customizing sewing workshops.

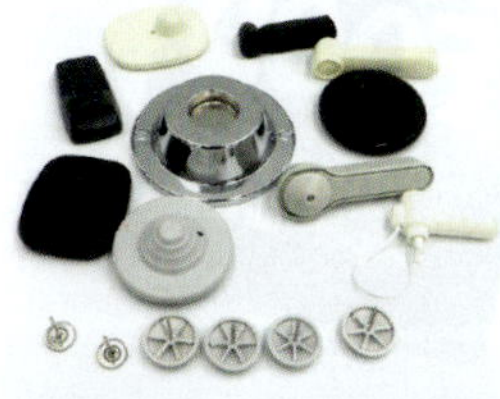

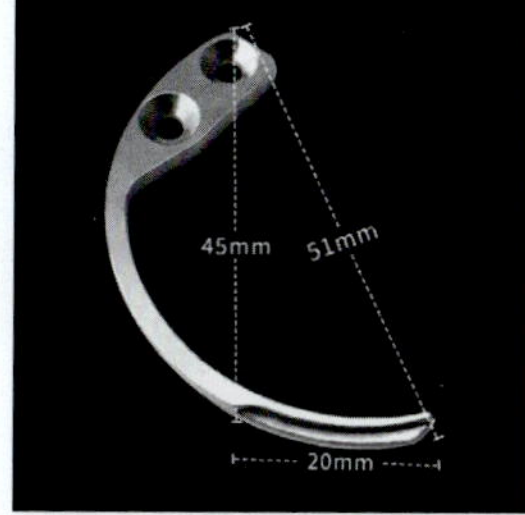

Contemporary tools for shoplifting.

A Digger doles out food in the Golden Gate Park Panhandle. The diggers used to give away free meals made out of dumpstered or stolen food every week. At the meetings, they took advantage of the occasion to read political poetry or hand out mimeographed pamphlets.

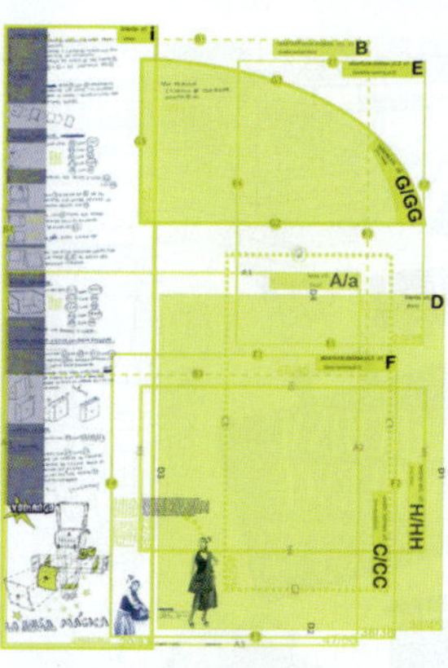

Instructions for making a "magic-bag" or also called "booster-bag" by Yomango.

Members "Los Solidarios". From left to right: Francisco Ascaso, Buenaventura Durruti and Gregorio Jover. They carried out bank expropriations in Spain, France, Uruguay and Argentina.

Illustration of the robbery of Société Générale Bank by The Bonnot Gang in Chantilly on March 25, 1912. The Bonnot Gang was one of the first affinity groups that started to do bank robberies with automobiles.

Coverage of the arrest of the band members of the Forty Elephants in the press.

The Night Workers was a group of anarchist thieves who specialized in burglary. Among its members was Alexander Marius Jacob, who left an important written legacy to comprehend his ethical motivations that led him to theft. Night Workers - Le petit journal 1901.

Conjectural map of a mediaeval English manor. The part allocated to 'common pasture' is shown in the north-east section, shaded green. Enclosure laws allowed landowners to fence off land formerly used as common pasture.

Point Blank! Situationist poster - Point Blank! was a situationist group from San Francisco who were active in the 70s.

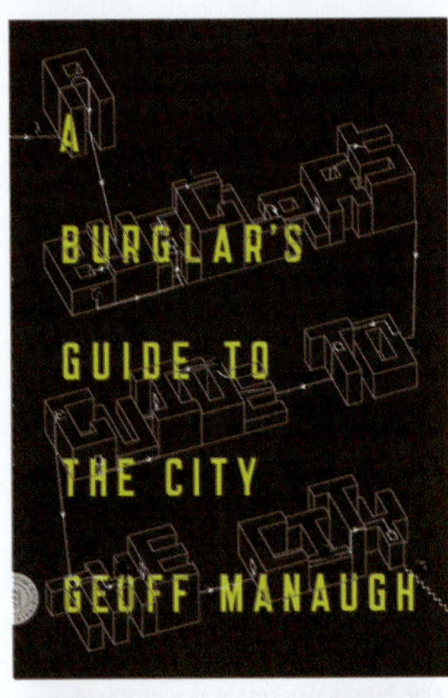
A
BURGLAR'S
GUIDE TO
THE CITY
GEOFF MANAUGH

ANARCHISM & VIOLENCE
Severino Di Giovanni in Argentina 1923 - 1931
by OSVALDO BAYER

GONE SHOPPING
The Story of
Shirley Pitts
Queen of Thieves

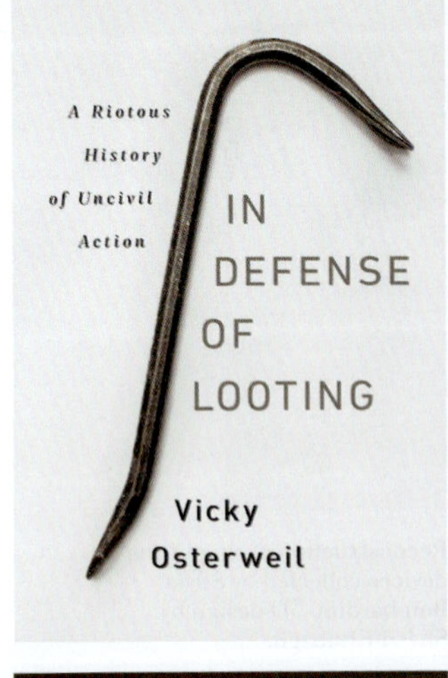
A Riotous History of Uncivil Action
IN DEFENSE OF LOOTING
Vicky Osterweil

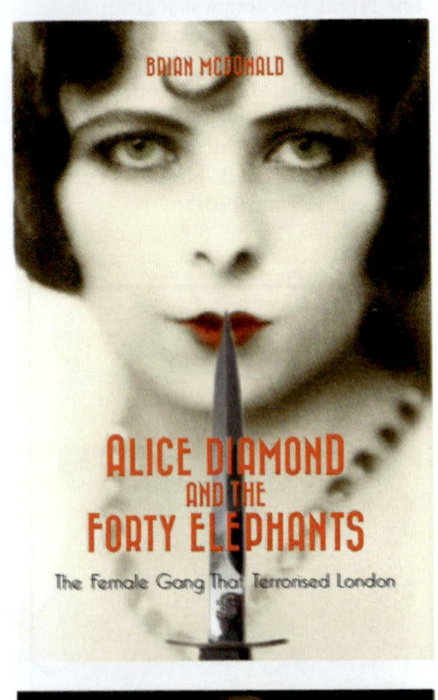
BRIAN McDONALD
ALICE DIAMOND AND THE FORTY ELEPHANTS
The Female Gang That Terrorised London

E. J. HOBSBAWM
BANDIDOS
ariel

How To
STEAL FOOD
From The Supermarket

NON REGOLARI
BERNARD THOMAS
LA BANDA BONNOT
FORUM EDITORIALE MILANO

SHORT STORY
FYODOR DOSTOYEVSKY
An Honest Thief

Eleuterio Sánchez
CAMINA O REVIENTA
Memorias de «El Lute»
Círculo de Lectores

SUPERUOMO : E : ICONOCLASTA
RENZO NOVATORE
Verso il Nulla Creatore

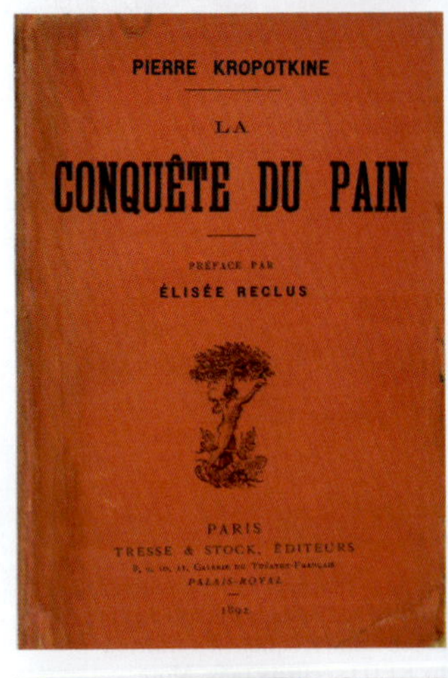
PIERRE KROPOTKINE
LA
CONQUÊTE DU PAIN
PRÉFACE PAR
ÉLISÉE RECLUS
PARIS
TRESSE & STOCK, ÉDITEURS

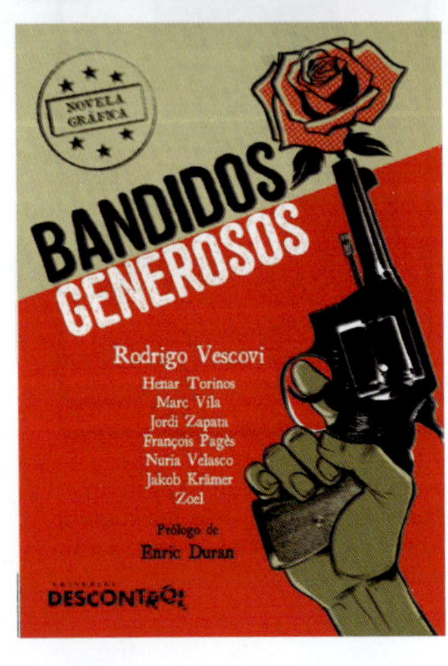
NOVELA GRÁFICA
BANDIDOS GENEROSOS
Rodrigo Vescovi
Henar Torinos
Marc Vila
Jordi Zapata
François Pagès
Nuria Velasco
Jakob Krämer
Zoel
Prólogo de
Enric Duran
DESCONTROL

Cómo expropiar a los bancos
Com expropiar als bancs
Manual bilingüe
castellano/català
melusina[sic]

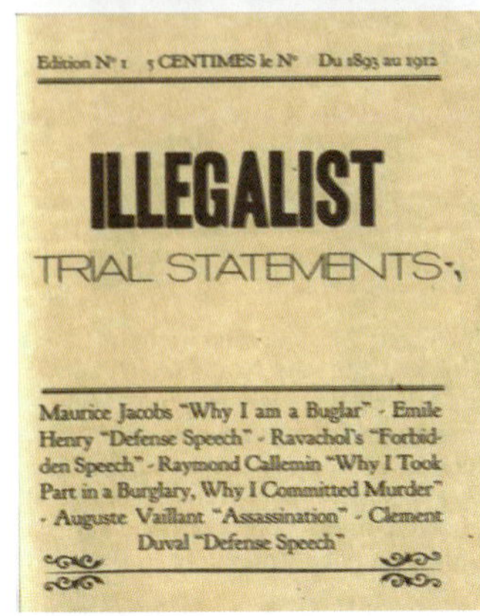
Edition N° 1 5 CENTIMES le N° Du 1893 au 1912
ILLEGALIST
TRIAL STATEMENTS
Maurice Jacobs "Why I am a Buglar" - Emile Henry "Defense Speech" - Ravachol's "Forbidden Speech" - Raymond Callemin "Why I Took Part in a Burglary, Why I Committed Murder" - Auguste Vaillant "Assassination" - Clement Duval "Defense Speech"

LIFTING
—THEFT IN ART

MI UTOPÍA VIVIDA
Lucio Urtubia

SHOPLIFTING
01/08/01 9:37 PM
SOCIAL HISTORY
KERRY SEGRAVE

THE ANARCHIST EXPROPRIATORS
BUENAVENTURA DURRUTI AND ARGENTINA'S WORKING-CLASS ROBIN HOODS
OSVALDO BAYER

A CULTURAL HISTORY of SHOPLIFTING
THE STEAL
RACHEL SHTEIR

Pirate Utopias
MOORISH CORSAIRS & EUROPEAN RENEGADOES
PETER LAMBORN WILSON

Abbie Hoffman
steal this book

THE EXTRAORDINARY ADVENTURES OF ARSENE LUPIN, GENTLEMAN-BURGLAR
MAURICE LEBLANC

THE THIEF'S JOURNAL by Jean Genet
"The most beautiful book that Genet has written."—Jean-Paul Sartre

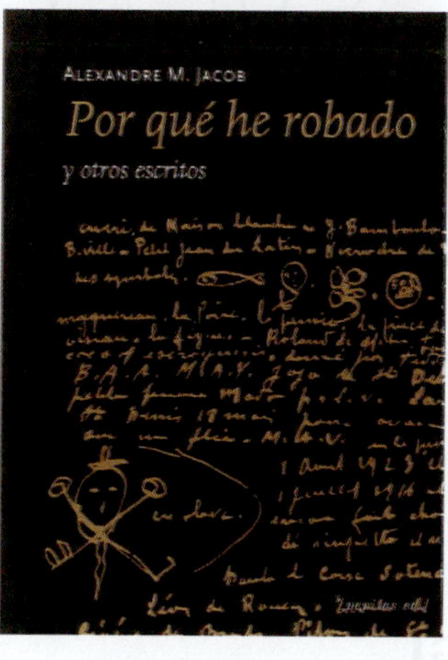
ALEXANDRE M. JACOB
Por qué he robado
y otros escritos

STEAL THIS COMPUTER BOOK 4.0
WALLACE WANG

THE GIFT
The Form and Reason for Exchange in Archaic Societies
MARCEL MAUSS

When Ladies Go A-Thieving
Middle-Class Shoplifters in the Victorian Department Store
Elaine S. Abelson

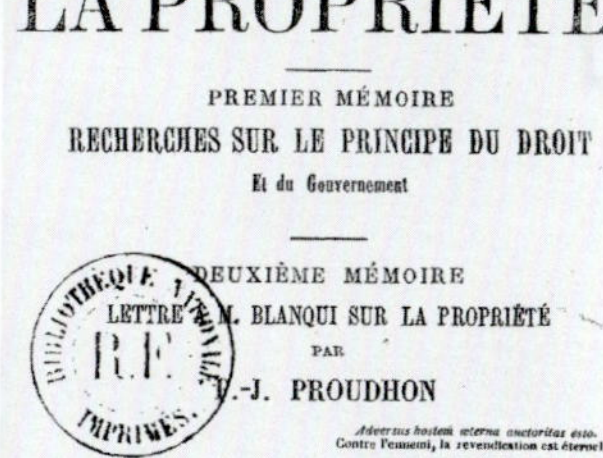
ŒUVRES COMPLÈTES DE P.-J. PROUDHON
(TOME I)
QU'EST-CE QUE
LA PROPRIÉTÉ
PREMIER MÉMOIRE
RECHERCHES SUR LE PRINCIPE DU DROIT
Et du Gouvernement
DEUXIÈME MÉMOIRE
LETTRE A M. BLANQUI SUR LA PROPRIÉTÉ
PAR
P.-J. PROUDHON
NOUVELLE ÉDITION
PARIS
LIBRAIRIE INTERNATIONALE
A. LACROIX ET Cie. ÉDITEURS

STOP, THIEF!
THE COMMONS, ENCLOSURES, and RESISTANCE
PETER LINEBAUGH

El Libro Morao
YOMANGO
WINONA dice: "Con este libro te pondrás morao"

THE PIRATE BOOK
READ ME

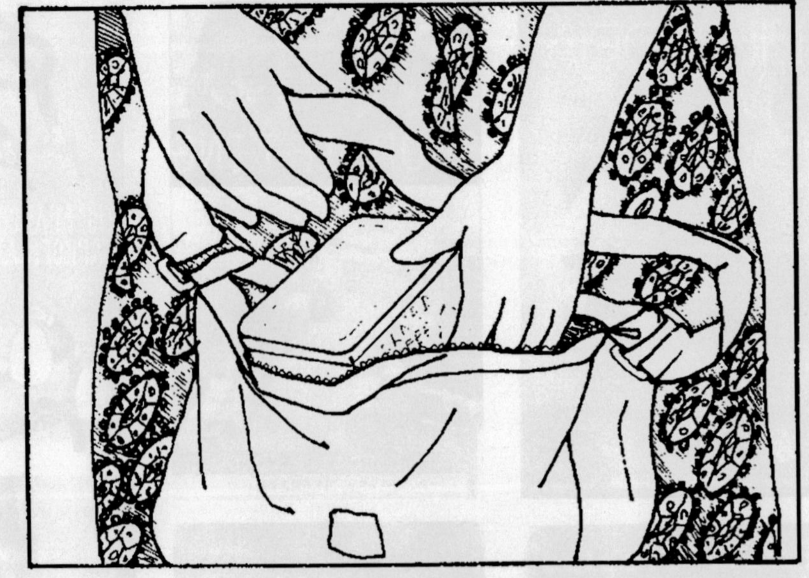

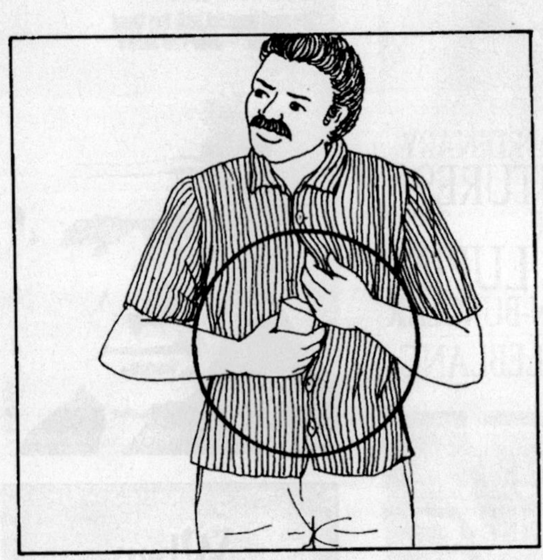

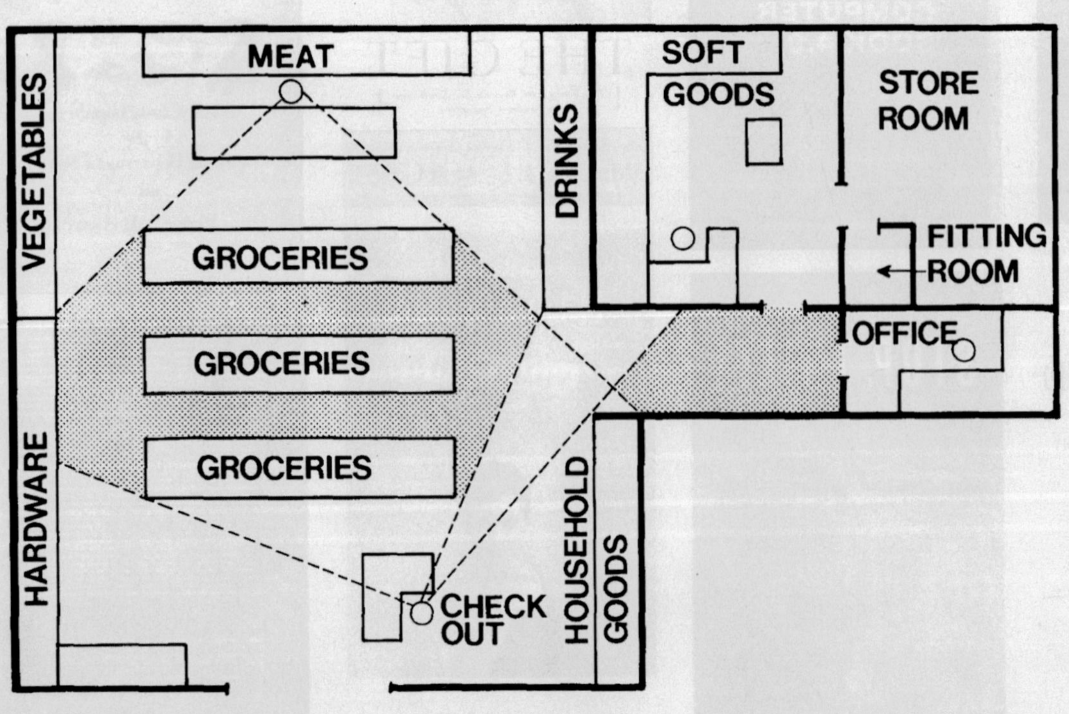
MEAT
VEGETABLES
GROCERIES
GROCERIES
GROCERIES
HARDWARE
DRINKS
SOFT GOODS
STORE ROOM
FITTING ROOM
OFFICE
CHECK OUT
HOUSEHOLD GOODS

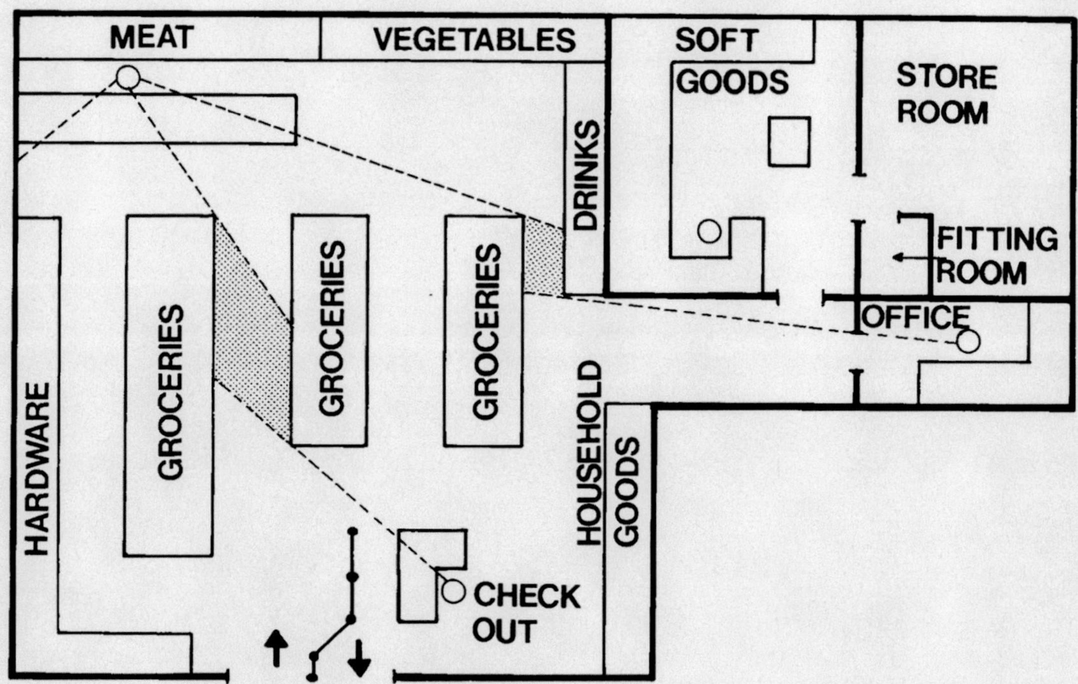

Pictures from the Matcom Retail shoplifting manual, funded by the Swedish government in 1978 and titled "Shoplifting - a learning element for staff of consumer cooperatives"

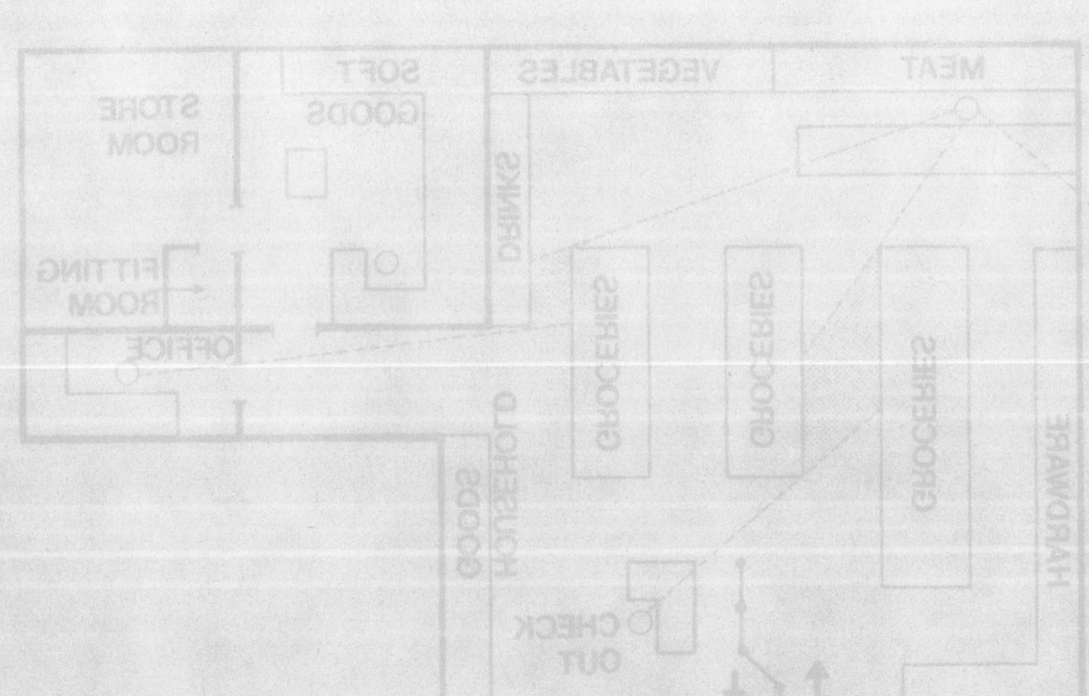

CUMBIA
AMANTES
DEL
SONIDO

KUMBIA
CALOR

TROPIKAL
ANDINO
666
36
IO-501
PURO SENTIMIENTO